TRADITIONAL COUNTRY LIFE RECIPE SERIES

CRANBERRY COMPANION

TRADITIONAL COUNTRY LIFE RECIPE SERIES

CRANBERRY COMPANION

Recipes by Liz Clark
Cranberry History by James W. Baker

Interior illustrations provided by
James W. Baker

Cover illustration by
Lisa Adams

The Brick Tower Press ®
1230 Park Avenue, New York, NY 10128
Copyright © 2004
by Liz Clark

Clark, Liz
The Traditional Country Life Recipe Series:
Includes Index
ISBN 1-883283-28-0, softcover

Library of Congress Catalog Card
Number: 2003109375
First Edition, September 2004

TABLE OF CONTENTS

Picking Cranberries Cape Cod Mass.
(1913 postcard)

Dedication

For my mother, the late Margaret Ruhl Clark, who never could have imagined a holiday table without cranberries.

Acknowledgements

First and foremost, Liz needs to thank John Warfield who tolerates her forays and willingly chauffeurs her to such destinations as the cranberry bogs on the "wilds" of Cape Cod. A very special "thank you" to P. T. Thorndike, long-time Massachusetts "foodie" correspondent, who put Liz in touch with Monica and Keith Mann, to whom she owes her understanding of cranberry culture "from the ground up." Their collection of antique cranberry equipment is both beautiful and insightful. Thanks also to food buddy Will Weaver whose encyclopedic knowledge of food history is always "just a phone call away"!

THE STORY OF AMERICA'S CRANBERRIES
by *James W. Baker*

THE HISTORIC CRANBERRY

Cranberries are more American than apple pie. It wouldn't be Thanksgiving without cranberry sauce, and Christmas dinner in America would be incomplete without the traditional cranberry condiment. Yet while the Pilgrims undoubtedly brought a memory of apple pie (and apple pie memories were all they had in 1621) to the "First Thanksgiving," they weren't having similar thoughts about cranberry sauce. Neither written nor oral tradition can enlighten us whether the berries played any role at all in that famous three-day feast in 1621, and if they did, it wasn't in the form of our familiar sweet sauce.

Cranberries have played a supporting role in American cuisine for so long that we take the familiar dark red fruit for granted, vaguely assuming that they were eaten from the time Plymouth Rock was still news. However, unlike the starring roles enjoyed by corn, pumpkins, and turkeys in the colonial records, cranberries humbly avoided the spotlight of history. They crept into colonial life unheralded, and appear incidentally in early records with no mention as to their first discovery or use.

The first mention of the cranberry in New England appears in John Eliot's *The Day-Breaking If Not the Sun-Rising of the Gospel with the Indians in New-England* (1647):

> "4. Quest. Their fourth Question was, How it comes to passe that the Sea water was salt, and the Land water fresh. Answ. 'Tis so from the wonderfull worke of God, as why are Strawberries sweet and Cranberries sowre, there is no reason but the wonderfull worke of God that made them so. (A Berry which is ripe in the winter and very sowre, they are called here Bearberries.)"

Eliot mentions in a second pamphlet (*The Cleare Sun-shine of the Gospel, Breaking Forth upon the Indians in New-England*, 1648) that the Indians sold "craneberries" in the spring and autumn, "and they find a good benefit by the market." Cranberries do not turn up in the Plymouth Colony records until 1651 when they are the incidental cause of a domestic tragedy; the death of John Slocume, a nine year-old boy:

> "Taunton, June the 10, anno 1651... on the 25t of Febreuary last [1650], the said John, goeing with a companie of persons, to the number of twenty, unto a pond called the Fowling Pond, about two miles from the towne, to gather cramberies, in his returning made some stay behind ye said companie, about a mile from his home, upon confidence of his knowlidge of the way home, being nine yeares of age, but mising the path, strayed in the woods, and returned not againe...his father...raised the towne, and with a

considerable companie the whole night following, with drum, guns and loud voyces, and 3 daies after with great dilligence sought him, but could not find him.

"… the 5t of January, that John Lincolne, in his following of cattle, found the skull of the said John, having his braine not wholly consumed; and January the 9th, found some other parts of the corpse, with part of his clothes scattered in smale peeces… wee doe apprehend that the said John, when hee strayed away, wandred with much labour, and being spent with wearines and cold, perished among the brushy shrubs and was devoured and torne, and the parts of his carkeis despersed with ravenus creatures."

These chance references indicate that the cranberry was part of the New England diet by 1650. We do not know how they were used–it is very unlikely that cranberry sauce became popular until sugar became more affordable later in the seventeenth century. Sugar had been an expensive ingredient in English cookery when the only source was from the Mediterranean countries. Once the English established their own sugar plantations in the West Indies, the price dropped to affordable levels. Jams and preserves, which had earlier been restricted to rich people and invalids (sugared preserves were considered medicinal), became common in England and the colonies. But how then did the cranberry enter into the cookery of colonial New England?

Actually, the cranberry, like the turkey and the pumpkin, was not entirely unknown to the colonists before they left England. A smaller variety of cranberry was found in England in certain localities, where it was known under the name of "Fen Whortes" or "Marrish [marsh] Whortes." Myles Standish had in his small library a copy of Lyte's translation of Rembert Dodoen's *A Nievve Herball*, or *Historie of Plantes* (1578), which has a description of the genus *Vacinia* or "whortleberries"–a classification which includes blueberries, huckleberries, and cranberries.

"Amongst these Whortes or Whortelberries we may recken those whiche the Germaynes or Almaignes doo call Veenbesien, that is to say Marishe or Fenberries, of which the stalkes be smal, short, limmer [limber] & tender creeping and almost layde upon the grounde, beset and deckt with smal narrow leaves, fashioned almost lyke to the leaves of the common Thime, but smaller, the berries grow upon very smal stemmes at the end or toppe of the litle branches, almost lyke the red Whortes, but longer and greater, of colour sometimes all red, and sometimes red speckled, in taste somewhat rough and astringent…Whortes growe in certayne woods of Brabant and Englande… Marrishe or Fen

Bog Houses were where itinerant workers bunked during their seasonal work on the cranberry bogs.
"Bog House," from James Webb's Cape Cod Cranberries, *New York, Orange Judd Co., 1907, p. 33*

Whortes growe in many places in Holland, in low, moyst places."

The accompanying woodcut of *Vacinia palustria* is an easily recognizable image of the cranberry. The name "cranberry" (or "cramberry") rather than "fen whort" was used from the beginning in New England, although it is unclear how this occurred. The popular folk etymology that it was suggested to the colonists by the suppositious resemblance of the cranberry flower to the head and neck of a crane is unlikely. As the name is a translation of the Dutch "kranebere," perhaps the term came from New Amsterdam or even from the Dutch experience of the Plymouth Pilgrims.

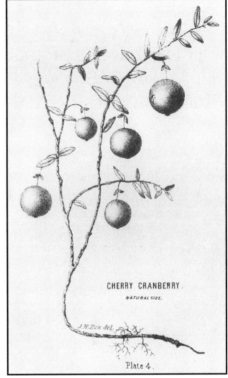

Woodcut of Cherry Cranberry (plate 4) from Eastwood (1860)

The Native Americans not only introduced the American cranberry to the New England colonists but also kept them supplied with the wild berries. It is possible that the "tenn barrells of cranburys" that were among the local produce sent to appease King Charles II in 1677 were gathered by Native People and traded to the English. The colonists' use of the cranberry, however, followed European precedents. It is often assumed that the colonists adopted many of the recipes of their Native neighbors, but there is little indication that this was the case. Certainly the Native Peoples contributed several new and unfamiliar ingredients to colonial cuisine, but most surviving colonial recipes seem to follow English rather than Native tastes. Connie Crosby, in "The Indians and the English use them much…" suggests that the cranberry may have recommended itself as a substitute for the English gooseberry or barberry in preserves and sauces. Almost forgotten today as an ingredient in Anglo-American cookery, the common "shoe peg" barberry was a common ingredient in seventeenth-century sauces and preserves because of its acidic flavor and red color. The first cranberry recipes are quite similar to earlier barberry recipes, and they add the same touch of tart redness to a dull-colored and dull-flavored dinner. Thomas Dawson gives a recipe for barberry conserve or sauce in his *Second part of the good Hus-wives Iewell* (London 1597):

"To make a conserve of Barberies
Take your Barberies and picke them cleare, and set them over a soft fire, and put to them Rosewater as much as you thinke good, then when you thinke it be sodde enough, straine that, and then seeth it againe, and to every pound of Barberies, one pound of suger, and meat your conserve."

Recipes for both barberries and cranberries are found in the first American cookbook, Amelia Simmons' *American Cookery* (1796). She also recommends serving roast turkey with "boiled onions, cramberry sauce, mangoes, pickles or celery."

As in the case of the strawberry, the American species of cranberry proved to be larger and more impressive than the European sort. John Josselyn, who spent over nine years in New England, provided a good description of the cranberry in 1672:

"Cran Berry, or Bear Berry, because Bears use much to feed upon them, is a small trayling plant that grows in Salt [sic] Marshes that are over-grown with Moss; the tender Branches (which are reddish) run out in great length, lying flat on the ground, where at distances, they take Root, over-spreading sometimes half a score Acres, sometimes in small patches of about a Rood or the like; the Leaves are like Box, but greener, thick and glistering; the Blossoms are very like the Flowers of our English Night Shade, after which succeed the Berries, hanging by long small foot stalks, no bigger than a hair; at first they are of a plane yellow Colour. Afterwards red and as big as a Chery; some perfectly round, others Oval, all of them hollow, of a sower astringent taste; they are ripe in August and September.

"For the Scurvy
They are excellent against the Scurvy.

"For the heat in Feavers.
They are also good to allay the fervour of hot Diseases.

"The Indians and English use them much, boyling them with sugar for Sauce to eat with their Meat; and it is a delicate Sauce, especially for roasted Mutton; Some make tarts with them as with Goose Berries."

Until the 19th century, cranberries were a wild fruit which people picked as they might. The berries were not restricted to New England– there were plenty of them to be had in New Jersey, and they were found by pioneer emigrants heading west into Wisconsin, Washington, and Oregon. In the late 1860s, stories spread around Berlin, Wisconsin, about the wealth that picking wild cranberries could bring. An Irish family, the Careys, hired poor men and women to pick cranberries by the bushel, which they then sold on the Chicago market. The family was said to have cleared $100,000. However, the most important development in cranberry production occurred first on Cape Cod, in 1816. Henry Hall, a Nobscusset (North Dennis) farmer began the practice of transplanting cranberry vines into special "cranberry yards." Other Cape farmers who had already been supplementing their income with wild berry harvests followed suit. By 1854, when cranberry culture was reaching beyond the Cape to Plymouth, Essex, Middlesex, and Norfolk counties, there were 197 acres of cranberry bog under cultivation in Barnstable County. This increased in ten years to 1,074 acres, and the national market for the tart red fruit began to grow, helped by a fashion for cranberry sauce among the wealthy elite.

A cranberry boom occurred in the 1850s and 1860s. Cape Cod and New Jersey residents discovered that useless acres of huckleberries and brush in the "pine barrens" were actually just what this valuable crop needed. After generations of trying to wring a meager living from the sandy soil, farmers found they could turn the local meadows and scrubby areas into profitable cranberry "yards" or bogs.

IN FROM THE WILD – CRANBERRY CULTIVATION

The cranberry is an agricultural contrarian–conditions that would doom other crops makes the cranberry healthier and more productive. Rather than rich loam, the cranberry prefers coarse sandy dirt over a boggy or salt marsh base. Where other plants require fertilizers, cranberries thrive on more sand. A flood will kill most crops; cranberries benefit from a layer of water and ice, which kills weeds and pests and, most importantly, protects the vines from harsh winter conditions. Growers take advantage of the winter ice to go over the bog and evenly spread a layer of sifted sand which will fall to the vines with the spring thaw. The main weakness cranberries share with other crops are weeds and insect pests. Sanding, flooding and hand-weeding help a great deal and sustained profitable harvests for many years, although labor costs have removed the latter as a practical alternative to herbicides and pesticides.

In the first book on cranberry cultivation, Benjamin Eastman's *The Cranberry and Its Culture* (1856), it is clear that there was a lively debate about

Cranberry Pickers on Cape Cod
(1900 real photo postcard)

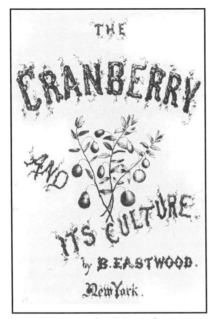

Eastwood's "Cranberry Culture" engraved title page from Benjamin Eastwood's A Complete Manual for the Cultivation of the Cranberry, *New York C.M. Saxton, Barker & Co., 1860*

what was the best way to grow cranberries. Some favored upland planting and others preferred bogs; some growers thought rich soil an obvious choice, or clay, or plain peat. One farmer might plant his yards with sods cut from a natural bog, and others used cuttings poked into the soil. Eastman approached berry cultivation from the combined experience of the Cape Cod growers, and recommended most of the practices that became standard in later years except perhaps for his opinion that sloping grounds were best for drainage.

Building a bog began with the clearing of a likely spot. The brush and weeds were mowed, and the turf cut and removed. The ground was then sanded and leveled, and drainage ditches dug; one or more deep, central ditches with smaller side ditches running perpendicular to the main channels. Cranberries require lots of water for irrigation in addition to the annual flooding, and the ditches provided this. A ditch was also dug around the perimeter of the bog, and banks or dikes built up to control flooding. Turf sods were built into solid walls around the bogs in New Jersey while sandy banks were preferred in New England. Floodgates or flumes were installed in these barriers to control the supply of water from adjacent streams and ponds.

Vines were then planted, usually in the spring on Cape Cod. Seeding wasn't very successful. Planting of vine-bearing sods, sections of vines or even chopped pieces of vines sown broadcast were the methods employed. The vine cuttings worked best. They could be set into the soil either by their middles with both ends sticking up, or in small bunches planted upright with their ends buried in the ground. The vines

"Cutting and Paring Turf" from Joseph J. White's Cranberry Culture, p. 53 (1870)

were carefully cultivated and the bogs improved by sanding and hand-weeding. It took several years for the bog to reach its potential, and it would quickly revert to a wild state if neglected.

The autumn harvest was the most labor-intensive part of the bog's cycle. Each fall, the bogs in southeastern New England employed large numbers of local folk as pickers. Whole families went out to the bogs (school attendance being excused in some towns) thoroughly bundled up against the sun, the cool mornings and the rough wet ground. As the industry grew, many more pickers came each year from distant parts for the hard-earned but welcome income the cranberry crop provided.

"Planting in Drills" from from Joseph J. White's Cranberry Culture, *p. 53 (1870)*

Among these itinerant laborers were the Irish, Italians, Syrians, and Slavs from Boston, Worcester and Brockton; and Portuguese, French-Canadians and others from New Bedford, Providence and Fall River. By the late 1890s. two ethnic groups would become the foremost hirelings in cranberry work in southeastern Massachusetts – the Finns and the Cape Verdeans.

Until recently, the houses erected for these temporary workers and their families could still be found around the local bogs but changing times and vandalism has largely done away with them. The ethnic workers themselves emigrated here, and their families have had three or four generations born in America. In Wisconsin, a similar situation occurred, save that Irish, Polish, and Native American workers assumed the effort of harvesting the berries.

The pickers were organized under supervisors who took care of such matters as dividing the bogs into picking rows marked off with twine, issuing the traditional six-quart tin picking pails and registering the picker's tally as they were measured into the field boxes in preparation for screening. They also made sure that the bog was picked clean and made their workers go back and get the berries they had missed. Until the 1890s when scoops came in to use, picking was all done by hand. Picking was hard work although a number of workers have left accounts of their pleasure at working out of doors in the golden New England autumn. Between the woody vines and scratchy weeds it was rough on the pickers' hands, but that didn't slow them down. The scoops speeded up the process and were used to the 1950s, although mechanical harvesters had already been in use for several decades.

Antique Cranberry Scoop from Plymouth, Mass. ca. 1898 (photograph)

Once the berries were measured and tallied, they were turned over to the screeners. Early screeners worked at table-height racks, or screens, about six feet long with slotted bottoms and 6-inch high board sides which sloped down at a slight angle. They were about three feet wide at the base end and tapered down to a 6-inch opening at the lower end. The berries were poured in at the base, and up to six people pushed them along so that the twigs, leaves, and smaller berries dropped through and the cleaned berries issued out of the opening into barrels. Later mechanical separators were used to clean the berries and remove the soft or bad fruit from the sound berries, although screeners continued to sort the berries by color and type. The machine made use of the "bouncing" principle– a good cranberry is solid and hard, and will bounce when dropped, while a soft bad one will not. The berries were dropped so that the good berries bounced onto

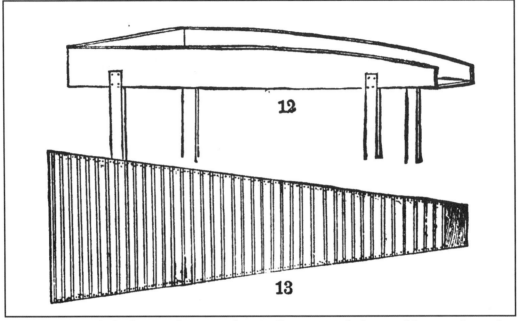

The screens (which were later mechanized) separated the good berries from the bad. The good hard berries bounced over the partitions where the rotten soft ones would not.

"Cranberry Screens and View of Bottom," from James Webb's Cape Cod Cranberries, New York: Orange Judd Co., 1907, p. 33

conveyors for screening and the bad berries fell into the reject container. The sorted berries were packed into barrels holding 100 pounds, which became the standard measure for sales. Even after actual barrels went out of use in the 1920s, wooden boxes were still graded as "half" or "quarter-barrel" containers.

Cranberry cultivation became increasingly scientific and mechanized in the 1930s and after. Gasoline water pumps, airplane dusters, and the big Mathewson picking machines were in use before the war, although much of the work on the bogs was still hand labor. The heavy reliance on labor became economically prohibitive during the mid-twentieth century and as in most industries, more and more mechanical and automated processes were introduced. The most important innovations have been the introduction of effective chemical pesticides, herbicides, and specialized fertilizers; the introduction of mechanized sprayers that could quickly wet or ice the vines, and "wet picking."

CRANBERRY ART

"Jersey Belle" brand New Jersey Cranberries (Eatmor)

At first, the brand names for these barrels and fractional-barrel boxes were like any other labels, using random images and pictures to differentiate the products of various commission houses and distributors. About 1912, however, the American Cranberry Exchange introduced an elaborate labeling system of grading and sorting of cranberries under their new "Eatmor" brand:

> "Under this system, berries were graded with almost scientific precision. The percent of coloration, keeping-quality, size, and variety were all factored together to determine the brand. For example, Skipper Brand was Early Blacks, averaging 75 colored with not more than 10 percent white colored; a count not over 150 to 150 per cup and fit for 15 days travel."

Eatmor came up with about 45 brands (not all marked with the company name) sharing a very distinctive design. The basic Cape Cod cranberry label had a gray or gray-green background with a distinctive image in the style of contemporary art nouveau posters. The New Jersey labels usually used color pictures on a yellow background.

Other independent growers and distributors used labels to identify particular crops or berries, but none were as detailed as the Eatmor label system. The labels became obsolete in the 1950s and 1960s as processing and pre-packaging made the brands irrelevant. They remain of interest to collectors, nevertheless, who value them for the artistic diversity within the basic Eatmor design. The present Ocean Spray gift shop on Water Street in Plymouth Massachusetts sells examples of the old labels to people who enjoy having examples of this bygone art, and examples turn up in the on-line Ebay auctions.

A THANKSGIVING TRADITION

On November 3, 1864, the Union League Club of New York resolved to "to co-operate in the movement in providing a Thanksgiving Dinner for Soldiers and Sailors at the front." The dinner given by the Club at the David's Island Army hospital for about 2,000 wounded or disabled patients was described as "in every respect equal to that furnished in our first-class American hotels. First came soup, oysters; then turkeys, chickens, roast beef, mutton, and other meats, with cranberry sauce, celery, and every variety of vegetable obtainable in the market; after this the pastry, and much of this was made by the best cooks in wealthy private families of the city; then apples, oranges, nuts, raisins, tobacco, and cigars, coffee and tea, as may have been preferred." This charitable drive drew donations in money of over $57,000 and in-kind gifts as well. Turkeys, cooked and on ice or on the hoof, made up the largest proportion of the in-kind donations, but there were also cranberry contributions which ranged from a single jar of berries from George Miller in Astoria, N.Y., to an entire barrel of cranberry sauce from a Mrs. Muller of the 21st Ward, New York City." This, the second of the national November Thanksgivings declared by Abraham Lincoln, helped establish our familiar holiday, and the cranberry was there! (See *Thanksgiving Cookery* by Elizabeth Brabb and James W. Baker, Brick Tower Press, New York, 1994 in this series.)

While it is doubtful that cranberries were present at the 1621 Plymouth harvest celebration we know as the "First Thanksgiving," they eventually became associated with that holiday and Christmas as well. As an autumnal product, cranberries joined other seasonal foods such as pumpkin, winter squash, potatoes, and turnips at the feasts, and their tart savor was made welcome at American tables. Some early American cookbooks such as Amelia Simmons *American Cookery* (Hartford, 1796, p. 18) or Mrs. E. A. Howland's *New England Economical Housekeeper* (Worcester, 1845, p. 72) specifically recommend that cranberry sauce be served with turkey, while others simply provide recipes for the sauce. It is difficult to know when the cranberry became indelibly associated with Thanksgiving as there are few references to the fruit in accounts of Thanksgiving dinners or on Christmas' bills of fare until the mid-19th century when cranberry sauce already seems to have been taken for granted. It is safe to say that cranberries are firmly lodged in Thanksgiving tradition from about the time of the Civil War. For example, in a collection of 254 Thanksgiving menus ranging from 1871

"Skipper" brand Cape Cod Cranberries (Designed ca. 1912)

The Eatmor Company used different labels to indicate the kind and quality of berries being shipped. Eor example, the "Skipper" label indicated Early Black berries of which an average of 75% were colored and not more than 10% were still white, with a count of not over 130 to the cup, and which could be safely shipped for 15 days of travel.

through the 1990s, only 18 do not list cranberry sauce. Some of these were from military units during wartime, but from 1944 on, all of the latter include cranberry sauce. In fact, cranberry sauce could be found in service menus in the Dominican Republic, China, Japan, Korea, Cuba, Iceland, Vietnam, and the Philippines, even if it was missing in California, Mississippi and London–or even in Washington State where the berries are actually grown!

CRANBERRY COMMERCE

The demand for cranberries at Thanksgiving and Christmas drove the trade for many years. The association with the holidays provided a guaranteed market that grew as more and more customers were convinced that they should include the berries in their holiday menus. However, this also fixed a seasonal limit to the cranberry market despite the fact that cranberries, if packed in plain water, could be effectively preserved for a far longer time than the four month window of holiday demand. Early home canning experiments suggested other commercial products. Yet although some cranberry jam and sauce was produced for sale, cranberries were sold primarily as raw fruit until well into the twentieth century.

Cranberry growers, like most other American agricultural producers in the 19th century, were organized in cooperatives which helped the individual members bargain with powerful wholesalers and suppliers. The first such group was formed in New Jersey in 1864. Joined with another New Jersey group, they became the American Cranberry Growers' Association in 1873. The Cape Cod Cranberry Grower's Association was formed in 1888. These regional cooperatives competed for markets until efforts were made to bring them together, first under the Grower's Cranberry Company in 1895, and then in 1907 by the National Fruit

Exchange. This was the work of A. U. Chaney of Iowa, who united Wisconsin growers (the Wisconsin Cranberry Sales Company), Massachusetts growers (the New England Cranberry Sales Company) and New Jersey growers (the Cranberry Sales Company) in competition with the older Grower's Cranberry Company. They all merged in 1911 to form the American Cranberry Exchange. The Exchange simplified the growers' dealings with wholesalers, stabilized prices, and marketed the berries under the "Eatmor" label.

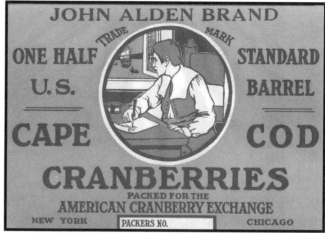

*"John Alnen" brand Cape Cod Cranberries
(Eatmor)*

Until the 1940s cranberries were usually sold loose from their wooden quarter-barrel boxes. Small cardboard scoops were sometimes provided to make it easier to measure out the berries for sale. Pre-packaged berries were introduced around World War II in one pound transparent bags and in cardboard boxes with cellophane "windows." The various dry picking methods we have been discussing produce cranberries which store well and can be sold in their natural state. However, an easier way to harvest the cranberry is to do so on a flooded bog with an amphibious machine that separates the fruit from the vines. The berries then float to the surface and can be "corralled" and sieved off the water for easy transfer to trucks and containers. These wet-picked berries do not last as well as the dry ones, but they are suitable for processing into juice or jelly. There is still a good market for dry-picked berries but the cheaper water-picked berries can be very profitable if processed into canned sauce, fruit juice combinations and other products.

The first recorded sales of preserved cranberries dates from 1828 when William Underwood of Boston wrote to Captain Stanwood of Augusta explaining the products his firm (of deviled ham fame) was shipping:

"The cranberries in the bottles are preserved without sugar. I name this because should any person purchase them for sweetmeats they would be disappointed. They are to be used precisely as if purchased fresh from the market, and will keep any length of time before the cork is drawn. Any English people will understand them, and

A.D. Makepeace advertising & packing materials (poster, box, and "Cape Cod Cranberries" sign, ca. 1940)

should you fall in with any Men-of-War they will be very agreeable for ships stores, for cabin use, and for any American families who wish for cranberry sauce. The cranberry jam is a sweetmeat and usually brings a high price. I have frequently sold it in India for $1.50 per jar."

The first cranberry-preserving factory was opened by a Mr. Randall in Wareham, Mass., in 1898, but it was in operation for only a few years. The actual beginning of commercial cranberry processing began in 1912 when Marcus Urann started canning cranberry sauce under the "Ocean Spray" label in Hanson, Massachusetts. John Makepeace ("Makepeace Cranberry Jelly") opened a cannery in Wareham, Mass., in 1928. Elizabeth Lee of New Jersey ("Bog-Sweets" brand cranberry jelly) was another pioneer canner. In 1930, Urann convinced the others to join a new processing cooperative, Cranberry Canner's, Inc., which marketed its products under the Ocean Spray label. In 1959, the company itself was renamed "Ocean Spray." By then the cooperative had become the dominant player in the national cranberry industry, absorbing rival organizations and representing growers in Wisconsin and on the west coast as well as Massachusetts and New Jersey.

Ocean Spray's First Cranberry Cocktail bottle, early 1930s (photograph)

Developing processed cranberry products was only half the battle. For many years the only commercial cranberry products in addition to the fresh berries were cans and jars of cranberry sauce, jelly, and juice. Dried or "evaporated" berries which could be boiled to make sauce enjoyed a brief popularity, especially during the war when they were provided to the U. S. Armed Forces. The cranberry industry also had to find a market for its products that went beyond the traditional holiday sales. The American Cranberry Exchange maintained a regular stream of complimentary cookbooks and other inducements to introduce the berries into everyday cuisine. By the 1950s, the use of cranberries and canned or bottled sauce spread beyond their original limited season.

It was with cranberry juice, however, that the business achieved its greatest success. Sales of cranberry juice and cranberry juice "cocktail" (diluted and sweetened) had begun in the 1930s. The product was initially sold in small pint or quart bottles, and marketed as a health benefit –"A Food–Not a Beverage," but it was a fruit drink that the juice succeeded. In the 1950s it was sold in a frozen concentrate and made available in gallon containers as its popularity grew. The big breakthrough came in the early 1970s when Ocean Spray decided to take advantage of the expanding American

Eatmor Cranberry's booklet,
44 Ways to Serve
the Tasty Fruit,
*American Cranberry
Exchange, 1930s*

demand for packaged fruit juice drinks. The entry into the juice drink market proved to be a tremendous success. The market took off, propelling Ocean Spray to unimagined sales and profits:

"… several cranberry-fruit blends have been successfully introduced to the public, and now over 90 per cent of the crop is sold as juice …Ocean Spray's recent growth has been beyond its founders' wildest dreams. One per cent of 1988's $800 million in sales revenue would have bought the entire cranberry crop in 1930, the co-op's first year of operation. In 1985 Ocean Spray broke into the Fortune 500."

Ocean Spray Cranberry label (ca. 1960)

The path to success has not been without pitfalls. Overproduction created crises among the growers as early as 1910. Another glut following World War II had disastrous effects on some growers. In 1959, another sort of disaster struck. The Food and Drug Administration released a report (15 days before Thanksgiving) that the berries were under suspicion as a cause of cancer because of the use of a pesticide introduced in 1957 called Aminotriazole. Although residues of the chemical only turned up a few West Coast consignments, the

Ocean Spray Cranberry label (ca. 1960)

government's warning resulted in a full-fledged panic, and sales plummeted. Various stores and restaurants removed cranberry products from their shelves and menus, and some cities banned sales altogether. The great Cranberry scare was one of the earliest "chemical" panics in the country, resulting from the FDA's policy adopted the preceding year, that any substance that causes cancer in lab rats in very high doses will harm humans at any level. The use of the pesticide ceased immediately and soon "contaminant-free" products appeared on the nation's shelves.

It took a while for the industry to recover from each of these set-backs, but the volatile nature of the industry continued. The great increase in cranberry profits mentioned above continued unabated into the 1990s. As sales boomed, growers eagerly increased the acreage of bogs in production and new growers entered what appeared to be a never-ending sellers' market. In 1997, prices for cranberries spiked to $80 a barrel, with an average of $66.20 (with the average cost of production at $44.10 per barrel). Reality returned in 1998 as the glutted market dropped the price to $37.50. Demand was still increasing moderately but production had completely outstripped it. Part of the reason was the decision of the Wisconsin-based Northland Cranberry Company to leave the Ocean Spray cooperative (which had always taken steps to prevent over-production among its members), and set up in competition to grow as many berries as possible for the then expanding market.

At present, (2000) huge surpluses have overwhelmed the market. Towns where cranberries are the main crop have seen dramatic drops in their tax revenues, and stories of bankruptcy swirl around the industry. However, this has happened before, and there is no doubt that the cranberry industry will survive this crisis. Cranberry products are as popular as ever in the American market and overseas as well. There is no question but that the humble berry of the bogs will once again rise above temporary set-backs and continue to provide its hearty red flavor in an ever-increasing number of ways.

Cranberry label (ca. 1960)

BUBBLES AND BOGGS

NOTE: *Keith and Monica Mann were largely responsible for Liz's understanding of cranberry culture–"from the ground up." Both are agricultural graduates of Cornell University, and Keith is a scion of a long-time Cape Cod cranberry growing family. After spending a day watching the dry harvesting of Monica's first organically transitioned bog, Keith, Monica, Liz, and John Warfield went to dinner at the Daniel Webster Inn in Sandwich, Massachusetts. The featured house cocktail was "Bubbles and Boggs," which of course was the appropriate starter for dinner that night!*

(1) Place the cranberry liquor into the bottom of a tall Champagne flute. Add the Champagne and serve immediately.

▧ INGREDIENTS

1 ounce of Boggs' Cranberry Liquor*

4 ounces of dry Champagne

* *Boggs' Cranberry Liquor is often difficult to find. If you cannot locate it, substitute cranberry schnapps or another cranberry liquor.*

MAKES 1 DRINK

CRANBERRY RUM PUNCH

NOTE: This smooth breakfast drink will belie the fact that it contains alcohol and, as Anne Wallace suggested in the cooking class, would be equally good warm at the holidays. Cranberry juice has fast become a notional favorite–full of vitamins and with a tart-smooth flavor, it's a great morning eye-opener.

(1) Place all of the ingredients into a cocktail glass or large wine glass and stir. Serve.

▨ INGREDIENTS

3 ounces of dark rum*
4 ounces of cranberry juice
3-4 ice cubes

* Cranberry juice completely hides the taste of the rum making it possible to do this drink with less than the most expensive of the dark Caribbean Rums. Liz would recommend such things as a medium priced Baccardi Dark. Highly flavored rums like Meyers' Dark would be lost against the cranberry juice. Save your money!

MAKES 1 DRINK

COSMOPOLITAN

NOTE: The most popular cocktail of the last decade has been the cosmopolitan. From the Rainbow Room to strip-mall Middle America, this drink took off with the trendy "cocktail revival." Here is a recipe from an excellent mixologist—Liz's friend Bill Foley, a resident of New York's West Village. Bill is the kind of perfectionist who keeps his liquors refrigerated so be forewarned that the ice does not immediately dilute this drink.

(1) In a shaker or mixer, combine ingredients, then shake with crushed ice and serve straight up with a slice of lime.

▣ INGREDIENTS

To make 1 cocktail:

1/4 part fresh lime juice
1/4 part Cointreau
1/2 part vodka
splash of cranberry juice for color

NOTE: Bill suggests adjusting the sweetness to taste by varying the proportion of Cointreau.

MAKES 1 DRINK

BLUE CHEESE WHEEL
WITH PECAN, DRIED CRANBERRY & CARAMEL TOPPING

NOTE: This showy appetizer makes a stunning centerpiece for a cocktail buffet, and replaces the over-worked baked brie of the past decade. It's guaranteed to bring raves from blue cheese lovers, and will serve a large crowd.

(1) Place the wheel of cheese on a baking sheet.

(2) Make a wreath around the top of the blue cheese wheel with the mixed cranberries and pecans. Leave the center of the wreath open, and allow about a 1/4-inch between the wreath and the edge of the cheese.

(3) Using a heavy pan with a pouring spout, if possible, make the caramel, watching it carefully so that it does not burn. When the caramel has reached the desired golden brown and smells caramelized, work quickly, pouring the molten caramel over the cranberries and pecans, allowing some to drizzle down the sides of the wheel of cheese.

⊠ INGREDIENTS

1 3-pound wheel of Maytag, or other quality blue cheese

1/2 cup of dried cranberries

1/2 cup of slightly toasted pecan halves

hot caramel made by melting 3/4 cup of sugar with 1/4 cup of water and allowing to darken to a maple-brown color, watching carefully, over high heat

(4) Be sure that all of the cranberries and nuts are glazed with the caramel. It will harden very quickly. Place the wheel of cheese on a serving platter and allow guests to serve themselves, cracking through the caramel to get some of the topping along with a wedge of cheese.

SERVES 24 AS PART OF A COCKTAIL BUFFET

CHICKEN LIVER PÂTÉ
WITH APPLES & CRANBERRIES

NOTE: The elegance and the mellow flavor of this appetizer pâté belie the simplicity of the ingredients. Even people who think they don't like liver-based pâtés will be seduced by the subtle underlying sweetness created by pureeing the apple with the liver. Sweet spices and dried cranberries are a surprise to the expected savory bite of most pâtés.

NOTE: If you have saved duck livers, by all means substitute them for the chicken livers. The unctuous combination of apples and duck liver is a perfect pairing.

(1) Combine the dried cranberries and cognac. Bring to a boil, remove from heat and cool. Melt half of the butter in a heavy enameled skillet over medium heat.

(2) Peel, core, quarter, and dice the apple.

(3) Add the onion and 2/3 of the apple and sauté until the onion is transparent. Add the chicken livers and sauté until just pink. (Do not overcook or liver can become unpleasantly bitter.)

(4) Drain the Cognac from the cranberries and add the Cognac to the skillet with the livers. Stir in all of the spices and sauté another minute, stirring constantly. Remove from heat and cool slightly. In a small enameled skillet, melt 2 tablespoons of the remaining butter. Sauté the remaining apple until it is just barely softened.

(5) Stir in the cranberries. Remove from the heat and cool.

INGREDIENTS

1/2 cup of dried cranberries
1/4 cup of Cognac or brandy
1/2 pound of butter
1 medium sweet onion, diced
1 large aromatic apple, peeled and diced
1 pound of chicken livers
1 teaspoon of salt
2 whole garlic cloves
1/2 teaspoon of cinnamon
1/4 teaspoon of allspice
1/4 teaspoon of ground ginger
1/4 teaspoon of white pepper

(6) In a food processor fitted with the steel blade, purée the livers with the remaining butter. Scrape the puréed mixture into a bowl and with a spatula fold in the sautéed apple and cranberries. Mix completely.

(7) Add salt to taste. Pack the mixture into a pâté dish; chill. Garnish the dish with a slice of apple, a sprig of mint, or an edible autumn flower such as a chrysanthemum. Serve with lightly toasted slices of French loaves and apple wedges.

SERVES 12 AS AN APPETIZER

PORK TERRINE
WITH FIGS AND CRANBERRIES

NOTE: Liz has served this terrine as a first course for dinner clients, accompanied by the Rhubarb/Cranberry Compote on page 43. She has also presented samples at food shows to surprised and pleased passers-by. Though French in concept, the cranberries make this a very American hors d'oeuvre or first course. If you have a Le Creuset pâté terrine it is the ideal cooking vehicle for this dish. If not, use small individual bread loaf pans and top them with aluminum foil, tied in place with kitchen twine.

(1) In the bowl of a food processor, fitted with the steel blade, chop the 1/4 pound bacon until fine. Add the ground pork, egg, onion, garlic, and all of the seasonings. (Do not put the figs and cranberries in the processor.) Pulse with several on/off switches of the processor to combine thoroughly. Remove the mixture to a bowl, and with your hands, mix in the plumped figs and cranberries and 1/2 cup of the port from plumping them.

(2) Line your pâté terrine or bread pans with the slab bacon, allowing the ends to hang over the outside of the pan. Shape the meat mix-ture into a log just long enough to fit into the terrine. Rap the pan down on the counter several times to settle the contents and remove any air pockets. Bring the over-hanging strips of bacon up over the top of the meat mixture to cover it. Place the bay leaves on top of the bacon and cover the terrine.

Preheat the oven to 350° F.

(3) Bring a kettle of water to a boil. Place the covered terrine or loaf pans in a roasting pan. Place the pan on the center shelf of the pre-

heated oven and pour boiling water into the roasting pan to come half-way up on the sides of the terrine. Bake for one hour, checking water level and adding more boiling water if it evaporates. After one hour, remove cover and check to see if surrounding liquid in the terrine is clear. If so, remove from water bath and cool, covered. Pour the liquid fat from the terrine and discard. Wrap a brick in aluminum foil and place on top of the cooled terrine. Weight over-night to compress into a firm loaf. Bring the terrine to room temperature and slice into 1/2 inch servings.

Do not skimp on the quality of your bacon. Buy the best you can find. Cheap bacon with artificial smoke flavor will ruin this dish!

▧ INGREDIENTS

1 pound of freshly ground pork
1/4 pound of high-quality slab bacon *
1 extra-large egg
1 medium yellow onion, peeled and chopped
2 fresh garlic cloves, minced
1 tablespoon of fresh thyme, minced
1/2 teaspoon of ground cinnamon
1/4 teaspoon of freshly grated nutmeg
1/2 teaspoon of freshly ground white pepper
1 teaspoon of sea salt
12 dried figs and 1/2 cup of dried cranberries covered with ruby port and simmered to reconstitute
1/2 cup of the port from plumping cranberries and figs, reserved
1/2 pound of slab bacon for lining the terrine
3 bay leaves
1 foil-wrapped clay brick for weight

SERVES 12

BUTTERNUT SQUASH SOUP
WITH CRANBERRY SWIRL

NOTE: The festive appearance of this golden soup with its brilliant red swirl of cranberry purée sets off any holiday table. Guests are greeted by it for their first course. Topped with a sprig of basil, it truly seems seasonal.

Preheat the oven to 350° F.

(1) Prick the squash with a sharp knife and place on a baking sheet. Bake until tender when pierced with a knife. Remove from oven and cool. Peel away skin and remove seeds. Dice flesh and reserve.

(2) In a heavy, enameled cast iron Dutch oven, melt butter over medium heat. Add onions and sauté until transparent but not browned. Stir in diced potatoes and cover the mixture with stock. Bring to a boil and add reserved squash. Reduce heat to a simmer and cook, stirring occasionally, until potatoes are soft. Cool the soup mixture. Purée in a blender until smooth. Add heavy cream and taste for seasoning, adding sea salt and cayenne pepper as needed. Garnish with a swirl of cranberry purée and a sprig of fresh basil in the center.

▨ INGREDIENTS

3 pounds of butternut or other hard autumn squash
8 tablespoons of butter
3 large yellow onions, peeled and diced
4 medium Idaho potatoes, peeled and diced
3 quarts of good quality beef or chicken stock (May use good quality bouillon.)
1 cup of heavy whipping cream
sea salt and cayenne pepper to taste.
Cranberry Swirl for garnish (see page 82)

SERVES 8

MIXED GREEN SALAD
HAZEL NUT OIL & CRANBERRIES

(1) Toss greens to mix.

(2) Pour over hazelnut oil and balsamic vinegar. Toss gently to coat greens.

(3) Add nuts, blue cheese, and cranberries.

(4) Season to taste with sea salt and freshly ground pepper.

❖ INGREDIENTS

6 cups of mixed baby greens; available in bins or bags in the produce department (Try to include the inner leaves of curly endive, arugula, radicchio for color, and inner leaves of romaine.)

3/4 cup of hazelnut oil (If unavailable, use extra-virgin olive oil.)

1/4 cup of cranberry vinegar (see page 83)

1/2 cup of blanched, lightly toasted hazelnuts, coarsely chopped

1/2 cup of crumbled blue cheese

1/2 cup of dried cranberries

sea salt and freshly ground pepper, to taste

SERVES 8

WALDORF SALAD
WITH CRANBERRIES

NOTE: This crisp apple salad was standard fare during Liz's childhood days at the farm. It made good use of the winter storage apples in the basement and was enriched by the hickory nut meats which Liz had picked out. Though contemporary "foodies" will cringe at the addition of miniature marshmallows, they were very much a part of the dish, as was the homemade sweet-sour boiled dressing.

(1) In a large bowl, combine all ingredients except lettuce leaves. Toss gently to thoroughly coat with the dressing.

(2) Mound the mixture in the lettuce leaves and serve.

▧ INGREDIENTS

1 cup of dried cranberries
6 large crisp red apples, cored, but not peeled, diced
1 cup of diced celery
3/4 cup of hickory nut meats
1 cup of miniature marshmallows
1 cup of Boiled Dressing (see page 79)
8 cup-shaped leaves of iceberg lettuce

SERVES 8

PORK CHOPS
WITH DRIED CRANBERRIES AND PORT WINE

(1) In a large flat plate, mix the flour, salt, cinnamon, and pepper. Dredge pork chops in the flour mixture.

(2) Melt butter in a heavy bottomed sauté pan over medium-high heat. Sauté chops in melted butter, approximately 3 minutes on each side, until nicely browned and caramelized. Remove chops from pan and place in a warming oven.

(3) Lower heat to medium-low. Drain all but 2 tablespoons of fat from pan. Pour in port wine, and with a square bottomed wooden spatula, scrape up all brown bits from the bottom of sauté pan. Add dried cranberries and allow port to reduce until syrupy, or until approximately reduced by half.

(4) Serve chops topped with cranberry port sauce.

⊞ INGREDIENTS

6 bone-in loin pork chops
1 cup of all-purpose flour
1 tablespoon of sea salt
1 teaspoon of cinnamon
1/2 teaspoon of cayenne pepper
8 tablespoons of butter
1 cup of ruby port wine
1/2 cup of dried cranberries

SERVES 6

COUNTRY HAM
RHUBARB/CRANBERRY COMPOTE

NOTE: *Wilma Day lives across the alley from Liz and is the best neighbor anyone could ask for! She pet-sits when Liz takes off—even for 2-month jaunts to Europe and her cutting garden keeps Liz supplied from spring to fall with fresh flowers for the dinner table whenever paying guests are coming. In the spring she brings a constant supply of fresh rhubarb.*

NOTE: *When Bill Rice, food and wine writer for the* Chicago Tribune, *and wife Jill, a recipe developer and cookbook writer, were coming for one of their bi-annual cooking class weekends with Liz, this country ham with the accompanying rhubarb and cranberry compote, was the main course for a dinner party to which Liz had invited many of Bill's and Jill's regular class participants.*

(1) In a large stock pot or ham boiler, submerge the pre-soaked ham in fresh cold water. Bring the water just to a simmer over medium-high heat. Reduce the heat and simmer for at least six hours, skimming the surface from time to time and adding fresh cold water as the liquid evaporates.

(2) Remove the ham to a carving board and discard the cooking liquid. To serve, trim the outside fat from the ham* and slice the flesh on the diagonal, to the bone.

⊠ INGREDIENTS

1 whole country ham weighing approximately 12 pounds, on the bone, soaked for 24 hours in several changes of cold water to remove some of the excess salt. (Scrub the ham well with a brush before soaking if any mold appears on the surface.)

SERVES 16-20 PEOPLE, OR MORE, IF PART OF A BUFFET

RHUBARB/CRANBERRY COMPOTE

(1) In a heavy enameled pan, (do not use exposed metal, as the acid from the rhubarb and cranberries will react with the pan) place all ingredients. Bring to a boil over medium-high heat. Reduce to a simmer, and cook, stirring frequently, until rhubarb has softened and cranberries have plumped. The compote should be fairly thick. Allow to rest for several hours in order for the flavor of the spices to penetrate the compote. Serve in a sauce-boat to accompany the sliced country ham.

▨ INGREDIENTS
3 large stalks of fresh rhubarb, washed and cut into 1/2-inch pieces
1 cup of dried cranberries
1 4-inch stick cinnamon
3 whole cloves
1 tablespoon of mixed whole white and black peppercorns and allspice berries**
1/2 cup of granulated sugar (or to taste)
water to cover

MAKES ABOUT 1 1/2 CUPS

Save the trimmed fat and the bone for some of the best bean or split pea soup you will ever make!

**Liz makes a mixture of 3 parts whole black peppercorns, 2 parts whole white peppercorns, and 1 part allspice berries, which she keeps in a pepper grinder. (This is available in French supermarkets where it is called "Melange de Moulin.")*

CHOUCROUTE GARNIE
WITH CRANBERRIES

NOTE: The cranberries are Liz's addition to this traditional Alsatian winter feast. Coming from the northeastern province of France, which borders on Germany, the German influence is strong in this dish, but the wine braising gives it a French accent. Smoked pork, a variety of sausages, and ribs all add up to a dish which can serve a crowd and hold for hours on a buffet table.

(1) In a large enameled cast iron Dutch oven, melt the lard over medium heat. Quickly sauté the sausages, chops, hocks, and rib racks. Remove the sausages, hocks, and chops and place in another kettle. Cover with water and allow to simmer.

(2) Add the pork butt to the lard and turn to brown on all sides. Meanwhile, continue to turn the rib racks. When the butt and racks are browned, add the onions, bay leaves peppercorns, juniper berries, and thyme. Cook until onion is transparent.

(3) Squeeze the kraut dry and add to the pork and onions. Cover with the wine and chicken stock. Return the smoked hocks to this mixture, reserving the sausages and chops. Stir the apples and cranberries into the kraut. Add more stock or water if mixture is not completely covered. Allow to come to a boil, then turn down heat and simmer for about 2 hours.

(4) Use the largest platter you can find and mound pork and kraut in the center. Surround with the reserved sausages and chops. Serve, accompanied by boiled potatoes and an assortment of mustards.

Fig. 14.—BOG-HOUSE.

INGREDIENTS

3 pounds of sauerkraut, rinsed under cold water, and reserved (Be sure you get the kraut in plastic bags from your meat department. Canned kraut is totally unacceptable!)

1/2 cup of lard

3 pounds of mixed sausages of your choice (mild flavors, not hot)

2 pounds of smoked pork hocks

2 pounds of smoked pork chops

3 pounds of pork butt

2 racks of baby back ribs, halved

2 large yellow onions, peeled and chopped

5 bay leaves

1 tablespoon of mixed whole peppercorns (black, white, and allspice)

20 juniper berries

1 tablespoon of dried thyme

3 cups of dry white wine

2 quarts of chicken stock

4 red apples, such as Jonathan, cored, but not peeled, quartered

1 12-ounce bag of fresh cranberries

SERVES 16-20

POT ROASTED CIDER BRAISED
PORK SHOULDER WITH CRANBERRIES

(1) Rinse the roast and pat dry. Season with salt and pepper. Dredge the roast in the flour.

(2) Melt the lard in a heavy bottomed, enameled Dutch oven over medium-high heat until the fat moves. Brown the meat on all sides. Don't worry if there is smoke —you want the edges of the meat to caramelize. Remove the meat and set aside.

(3) Add the onions and garlic and sauté until the onion is transparent. Add the bay leaves and the thyme. Deglaze the pan with red or white wine. Boil off the alcohol. Reduce the heat to low. Return the roast to pan and add the cranberries and cider. Cover and simmer for 3–4 hours or until the meat is tender.

(4) Remove the meat and cook the liquid down until it is a thickened sauce.

▨ INGREDIENTS

1 4-pound pork shoulder roast, bone-in
1 cup of flour
2 teaspoons of sea salt
1/4 teaspoon of freshly ground black pepper
1/4 cup of lard or enough to cover the bottom of the Dutch oven
2 medium onions, chopped
2 large cloves of garlic, minced
3 bay leaves
1 teaspoon of dried thyme
1/2 cup of good quality wine
1 cup of dried cranberries
1 quart of apple cider, unpasteurized, if possible

SERVES 8

VENISON TENDERLOIN
WITH CRANBERRY CREAM SAUCE

NOTE: Liz was inspired to prepare this recipe by a bottle of cranberry wine purchased at Iowa's Amana Colonies.

(1) In a heavy bottomed enameled skillet, melt the butter over medium-high heat. Pat venison dry with paper towels. Add venison to the skillet and brown on all sides. Meat should reach an internal temperature of 135° F. If it's a thick cut, after browning, the meat can be finished off in a 350° F. oven until it reaches the desired temperature.

(2) Remove the meat to a carving board and cover with foil to keep warm.

(3) Add the 3/4 cup of wine to the skillet and bring to a boil. With a square bottomed wooden spatula, scrape the bottom of the pan to remove any brown bits.

(4) Allow the wine to reduce by half. Add cream and cranberries. Bring to a boil. Reduce until the liquid coats the spatula. Season to taste with salt, nutmeg, and pepper.

(5) Slice the venison on the diagonal and fan out on warm plates. Top with the cranberry cream sauce.

▥ INGREDIENTS

2 tablespoons of butter

1 boneless venison tenderloin cut in half (about 1 pound of combined weight)

3/4 cup + 1 cup (see below) of cranberry wine (If unavailable, substitute Reisling.)

1 cup of whipping cream

1 cup of dried cranberries–simmered in 1 cup of the wine to plump

sea salt, freshly ground nutmeg, and white pepper, to taste.

SERVES 4

POT ROAST OF BEEF
CRANBERRIES, WALNUTS, AND RAISINS

NOTE: Slow, moist braising of less tender cuts of meat can eventuate in some of the most flavorful dishes which will arrive on your table. This top round of beef becomes meltingly tender when slow cooked with port wine and the dried ingredients, which become an elegant sauce when reduced down.

(1) Pat meat dry with paper towels.

(2) Mix together flour and salt and pepper on a flat plate. Dredge meat on all sides.

(3) Heat oil in a heavy-bottomed enameled Dutch oven over medium-high heat. Brown meat on all sides. Remove meat from pan and set aside. Lower heat.

(4) Add onion, garlic, bay leaves, and dried thyme. Cook, stirring constantly with a flat bottomed wooden spatula until onion is translucent.

(5) Add white wine and port to the pan and scrape the bottom with the spatula to loosen any browned bits. Return the meat to the Dutch oven and add the cranberries, walnuts, and raisins. Reduce heat to simmer.

(6) Add the bouillon. Cover. Cook, turning meat occasionally for three to four hours or until roast is fork tender. Remove meat to a carving board and cover with foil to keep warm.

(7) Raise heat and reduce wine and fruit mixture, stirring constantly, until it is quite syrupy.

(8) Slice meat and serve, passing the sauce in a sauce boat.

1 4-pound bone-in top round of beef

1/2 cup of flour

sea salt and freshly ground pepper, to taste

extra-virgin olive oil

1 large onion, peeled and chopped

1 tablespoon of minced garlic

3 bay leaves

1 tablespoon of dried thyme

one-fifth moderately priced, dry white wine

1 cup of ruby port

2 teaspoons of whole allspice berries

2 teaspoons of dried cranberries

1 cup of lightly toasted English walnuts

1 cup of dried Sultana raisins

1 cube of Knorr beef bouillon

SERVES 8

BRISKET
OF CORNED BEEF WITH LINGONBERRY GLAZE

NOTE: *Corned beef is not just St. Patrick's Day. In fact, it's not even Irish! The Jewish Ghetto was next to the Irish Ghetto in turn-of-the-century New York, and since Irish bacon was unavailable to the immigrants, they substituted Jewish Deli corned beef for the pork they were familiar with from the old country. Lingonberries are a northern European cousin of the cranberry. Tiny, but flavorful, these little berries have a great place in this recipe, as the basis for a glaze. Liz encountered them first in Finland, on her way to Russia in the mid-1980s. They are available as a jam or jelly in most supermarkets today.*

(1) Cook corned beef in simmering seasoned water for 3 1/2–4 hours. Add water as evaporation occurs, to keep brisket covered.

(2) When brisket is tender when pierced with a fork remove to a platter and cool.

Preheat the oven to 350° F.

Glaze

(3) Whisk together lingonberry jam and mustard. With a pastry brush, coat the top side of the cooled corned beef brisket with the lingonberry jam. Place the brisket on the rack of a roasting pan, glazed side up.

(4) Roast in the preheated oven for 20-25 minutes. Remove to a carving board and allow to rest for at least 10 minutes before carving. Slice across the grain into thin slices.

INGREDIENTS

1 pre-cured corned beef brisket
(about 3 1/2 pounds)
packet of seasoning for corned
beef or 3 tablespoons of
mixed pickling spices
cold water to cover

GLAZE

1/2 cup of prepared lingonberry
jam
2 tablespoons of stone-ground
Dutch mustard

ALTERNATIVE

(1) Cook the beef brisket then glaze,
following steps 1 through 3.
(2) Grill on a gas or charcoal grill,
preheated to medium-high, for 20-
25 minutes. Allow to rest and slice
as in step 4. Cooking in this man-
ner gives a great smokey taste to
the corned beef.

SERVES 8-10

ROAST GOOSE/CRANBERRY STUFFING

NOTE: Goose always presents a dilemma because of its high fat content. It is a very expensive bird (the average 10 pound goose will run you upwards of $40.00) so no one wants to ruin their investment by serving a greasy bird! The secret to this festive bird is to use two roasting pans! The first 1/2 hour of roasting, unstuffed, and untrussed, allows the excess fat to render from the bird and gives you the pure goose fat, which makes incredible fried potatoes and exquisite pastry.

Preheat the oven to 450° F.

(1) Place oven rack in the center of the oven. Spray a roasting rack with non-stick cooking spray. Place the rack in a heavy roasting pan large enough to hold the goose. Remove any loose fat from the cavity of the goose and place in the bottom of the pan. Place the goose, breast side down on the rack in the pan. Place the pan on the center shelf of the oven and roast for 30 minutes. Remove the goose from the oven.

(2) Prepare a second roasting pan in the same way. With two hot pads, firmly grasp the legs of the goose and lift it to the second pan. Place it on the rack, breast side up. Salt and pepper the cavity as well as the outside of the goose.

(3) Mix together all of the stuffing ingredients and fill the cavity of the goose. With kitchen twine tie the legs of the goose together, tucking the "Parson's nose" firmly over the stuffing and secure. Tuck the neck skin under the back and tie the skin and wings of the bird with a second piece of twine, securing them firmly to the sides and back of the goose.

(4) Return the stuffed goose to the 450° F. oven and immediately lower the temperature to 400° F. Roast for 45 minutes, then check the goose for browning. If skin is beginning to turn golden, lower the oven temperature to 375° F. and roast until the leg joint moves gently when jiggled, and the juices from

GIBLET GRAVY

Reserved neck, heart, and gizzard of
the goose
3 cups of chicken stock
1/2 cup of minced celery
1 medium yellow onion, diced
2 bay leaves
1 teaspoon of dried thyme
1/2 teaspoon of freshly ground pepper

(1) While goose is roasting, simmer all
ingredients for 1 hour. Strain
through a sieve and reserve stock,
neck, heart, and gizzard. Shred
meat from neck, chop heart and
gizzard, and return to stock.
Thicken with 1 tablespoon of corn
starch mixed with 1/2 cup of cold
water.

the thigh run clear when
pierced–about 30-45 minutes longer.
A meat thermometer should register
175° F. Remove from oven and
allow to rest for 30 minutes.

▣ INGREDIENTS

1 10–12 pound goose, thawed, rinsed
and patted dry–neck and giblets
reserved for gravy
non-stick cooking spray
sea salt and freshly ground pepper

FOR STUFFING

1 recipe corn bread–enough to make
a 9x9-inch square pan, cubed
12 ounce bag of fresh cranberries
2 firm red apples, cored, but not
peeled, cut into 1/2-inch cubes
2 large oranges, zest reserved, and
added separately, peeled and diced
2 large garlic cloves, minced
4 tablespoons of chopped fresh sage
2 tablespoons of chopped fresh
thyme
2 tablespoons, of chopped fresh
Italian parsley
3 extra-large eggs
2 teaspoons of sea salt
1 teaspoon of freshly ground pepper

SERVES 6

ROAST DUCK WITH CRANBERRY GLAZE

NOTE: The Clay roasting pot, or Romertopf, is Liz's favorite way of roasting a duck. It allows the fat to render without drying out the meat. Removing the top for the final half hour will allow the skin to crisp, while keeping a wonderfully flavorful bird.

(1) Fill the two halves of the clay pot with warm water and allow to soak for at least 15 minutes.

(2) Place the bay leaves and thyme sprigs in the bird's cavity, and lightly salt and pepper the bird.

(3) Drain the water from the pot and place the bird, breast side down, in the bottom half of the pot. Place the lid on the pot and put the pot on the center shelf of the oven.

(4) Turn the oven to 450° F. Allow to cook for 30 minutes. Remove the pot from the oven and turn the duck breast side up. Cover and replace in the oven.

(5) Roast for another 30 minutes. Remove the lid from the pot and continue to roast for another 30 minutes.

Glaze

(1) Whisk together all the glaze ingredients and simmer for 15 minutes. Mixture should be thick enough to paint on duck with a pastry brush.

(2) Brush duck with glaze and return to oven. Watch carefully. Glaze should just bubble but not burn. As soon as glaze begins to caramelize, remove duck to a carving board to rest for about 10 minutes before carving.

◼ INGREDIENTS

1 5-pound duck, thawed, rinsed,
  and giblets removed
sea salt and freshly ground pepper
2 bay leaves
6 sprigs of fresh thyme 4-inches
  long

GLAZE

1 cup of cranberry sauce (homemade or canned, see page 75)
2 tablespoons of orange marmalade
1/2 cup of reconstituted Knorr
  beef bouillon mixed with 1 cup
  of water
3 tablespoons of cognac or
  brandy
1 tablespoon of Dijon mustard

SERVES 4

SALMON WITH CRANBERRY HONEY

(1) Place the salmon skinside down on a baking sheet which has been covered with foil.

(2) Lightly salt and pepper the surface of the salmon with sea salt and freshly ground white pepper.

(3) Brush entire surface with honey, preferably cranberry honey if you can get it. Sprinkle entire surface with approximately 2 tablespoons of finely chopped fresh thyme.

(4) Bake in a preheated 400° F. oven or cook covered on a grill preheated to medium-high. Cook approximately 8-10 minutes to the inch of thickness, or until the fish turns slightly opaque but is still pink in the center. If desired, serve accompanied by a cranberry/orange/thyme relish (see page 77)

While attending the Cranberry Festival and watching the cranberry harvest on Cape Cod in October of 1999, in preparation for this book, Liz met Peter Wilson, a beekeeper who moves his hives from bog to bog during the spring to pollinate the cranberries. The resulting "cranberry honey" can be purchased from him at Cape Cod Cranberry Bog Honey, Peter C. Wilson, 56 Mayflower Ridge Drive, Wareham, Mass. 02571.

▨ INGREDIENTS

1 whole filet of salmon, skin on (approximately 2 1/2–3 pounds)
1/2 cup of cranberry honey
2 tablespoons of minced fresh thyme
sea salt
freshly ground white pepper

CRANBERRY & TANGERINE
POLENTA CROUTONS

(1) In a heavy enameled Dutch oven (one with a non-stick surface is ideal) bring three cups of the chicken stock, olive oil, and butter to a boil.

(2) Add the tangerine juice and zest; then cranberries.

(3) Whisk together the 2 cups reserved stock and cornmeal. Pour into the boiling liquid.

(4) Switch to a square wooden spatula and stir constantly, mashing any lumps which may form, against the sides of the pan. Continue to stir for about 8 minutes, or until mixture forms a thick porridge.

(5) Add the Parmesan cheese.

(6) Spray an 11x18-inch sheet pan with sides with non-stick cooking spray. Pour the polenta onto the sheet pan and smooth with a spatula. Allow to cool until firm. With a sharp knife, cut the cooled polenta into triangles.

(7) Preheat the broiler. Place the polenta triangles, without touching, on another sheet pan which has been sprayed with non-stick cooking spray.

(8) Place the sheet under the broiler and toast the polenta, watching carefully. When the tops are golden brown, turn and brown the under sides. Repeat until all of the polenta triangles have been browned.

CAPE COD CRANBERRY COCKTAIL

1 pint Cape Cod Cranberries
1 pint water   2 oranges   1 lemon   Sugar

Boil cranberries until skins break. Strain thru a sieve. Slice and press oranges and lemon, skins and all. Add juice to cranberry juice and strain thru a cloth. Add sugar to taste.

CAPE COD CRANBERRIES

BEATON'S DISTRIBUTING AGENCY
WAREHAM, MASS., U. S. A.

CAPE COD CRANBERRY MOCK STRAW-
BERRY SHORTCAKE FILLING

1 cup ground Cape Cod Cranberries
1 cup ground tart apples (Baldwins or Greenings)
¼ cup canned crushed pineapple
1 cup sugar   1 pinch of salt

Mix thoroughly. Let stand 2 hours and serve with your favorite biscuit or cake shortcake. Top with whipped cream.

BAKED CAPE COD CRANBERRY SAUCE

1 quart Cape Cod Cranberries
2 cups sugar

Wash cranberries and place in baking dish. Sprinkle sugar over them, cover and bake 20 minutes in a moderate oven (350°). If baked 1 hour in 275° oven cranberries will keep whole and practically candied.

PRINTED IN U. S. A.

▨ INGREDIENTS

5 cups of chicken stock (reserve 2 cups of stock to mix with cornmeal)
4 tablespoons of olive oil
1 stick (8 tablespoons) of butter
grated zest and juice of two tangerines
1/2 cup of dried cranberries
1 1/2 cups of yellow cornmeal (Grocery store cornmeal is just fine. Special polenta mix is not necessary.)
1 cup of freshly grated Parmesan cheese
non-stick cooking spray

SERVES 8-12 AS A SIDE DISH WITH ROAST POULTRY

GRATIN
OF BARLEY AND CELERY AND CRANBERRIES

NOTE: This healthy, tasty combination of grain and wonderfully antioxidant vegetables and fruits works equally well as a the stuffing for poultry instead of as a vegetable side dish. Liz is extremely fond of barley and finds it a much underutilized grain. It's nuttiness punctuates anything that it is served with.

(1) Cook the barley until soft and reserve. In a large skillet melt the 4 tablespoons butter over medium heat. Add the chopped celery, onion, and McIntosh apple and stir constantly with a wooden spatula until celery is soft and apple has virtually crumbled. Stir in the dried cranberries, thyme, salt and pepper. Add the reserved barley. Taste for seasoning. Spray a large gratin dish with non-stick spray and evenly spread the barley mixture in the dish. Top with the bread crumbs. parsley and butter mixture,

Preheat the oven to 350° F.

(2) Bake gratin in the preheated oven until crumbs have toasted and gratin is heated through. About 25-30 minutes.

▨ INGREDIENTS

2 cups of barley, covered with 3 cups of lightly salted water, brought to a boil and covered. Simmer until water is absorbed and barley is tender.

4 tablespoons of butter

2 cups of chopped celery, green leaves included

2 medium yellow onions, peeled and diced

1 large McIintosh apple, peeled and diced

1 cup of dried cranberries

1 teaspoon of minced fresh thyme

sea salt and freshly ground pepper, to taste

1 cup of fresh bread crumbs processed in a food processor with 1/4 cup of minced parsley and 4 tablespoons of butter

SERVES 8

SWEET POTATOES
WITH CRANBERRIES AND PEPPERS

NOTE: The savory combination of peppers, onions and cranberries gives a new dimension to the classic holiday sweet potato side dish; and no marshmallows! This is a very adult accompaniment to the holiday roast, but with just enough sweetness to please the entire family.

(1) Cover sliced sweet potatoes with cold water and add sea salt. Bring to a boil over medium-high heat. Reduce heat and simmer until just tender when pierced with a fork. Drain. Place sweet potatoes in one layer in a heavy baking pan which has been sprayed with non-stick spray.

(2) In a heavy skillet, melt the butter over medium heat. Add the onion and sauté until just transparent. Stir in peppers and continue stirring until they begin to soften. Add cranberries, bay leaves, brown sugar, and cinnamon. Cook, stirring constantly, until the cranberries begin to pop. Spread the cranberry-pepper mixture over the sweet potatoes.

Preheat the oven to 350° F.

(3) Place the baking dish on the center shelf in the preheated oven and

✪ INGREDIENTS

3 pounds of sweet potatoes peeled and sliced into 1-inch rounds
1 teaspoon of sea salt
4 tablespoons of butter
1 large yellow onion, peeled and diced into 1/2-inch pieces
1 cup of diced mixed colored peppers (red, green, yellow, and orange)
6 ounces of fresh cranberries
2 bay leaves
1/2 cup of light brown sugar
1/2 teaspoon of ground cinnamon
non-stick spray for coating baking dish

bake for 30 minutes. Remove from the oven and serve as an accompaniment to roast pork, turkey or beef.

SERVES 8

"MISS VICKI'S"
SWEET POTATOES

NOTE: *Vicki Miller is a hoot! A southerner by birth, with a terrific sense of humor, she was a long-time cooking class regular while living in Burlington, Iowa. Even when she and husband Al moved to Lexington, Kentucky, they made weekend returns coming as dinner clients on Friday night, and for cooking classes on Saturday morning. When Liz presented the preceding sweet potato/cranberry/pepper dish in a class on Antioxidants, an on-going joke arose about "marshmallow fluff" being a necessary ingredient in any sweet potato dish!*

NOTE: *At a Friday evening dinner, to which Al and Vicki had brought dinner guests, Liz could not resist creating the following sweet potato—complete with "marshmallow fluff"!*

Preheat the oven to 350°F.

(1) Cut the pointed tips off of the sweet potato halves, so that each half will stand up-right. With a lemon stripper or channel knife, cut a spiral all the way around each half from top to bottom. Rub each half with some of the softened butter and wrap tightly in the aluminum foil. Bake on the center shelf of the pre-heated oven until just tender, but not mushy when squeezed with an oven mitt. Remove the potatoes from the oven and unwrap. Using a melon baller, scoop the softened insides from the potato halves, leaving a 1/4-inch shell.

(2) Preheat the broiler.

(3) Mash together all of the ingredients except the "marshmallow fluff." Refill the potato halves with the mixture. Top each filled sweet

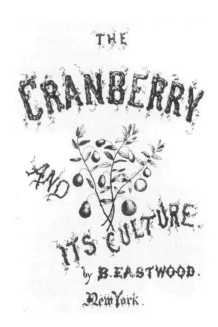

THE CRANBERRY AND ITS CULTURE.

by B. EASTWOOD.

New York.

potato with a tablespoon of "marshmallow fluff." Place upright on a cookie sheet and place under the preheated broiler. Heat until "fluff" melts and potatoes are warmed through. Serve immediately.

▣ INGREDIENTS

2 large, very straight, sweet potatoes, cut in half
2 tablespoons of butter, softened
4 squares of aluminum foil large enough to completely enclose the sweet potato halves

FOR FILLING

Flesh from the sweet potato halves
1/4 cup of toasted pecans, chopped
3 tablespoons of dark brown sugar
1/4 cup of dried cranberries, plumped in warm water and drained
4 tablespoons of softened butter
1/2 teaspoon of ground cinnamon
1/8 teaspoon of freshly grated nutmeg
sea salt and white pepper, to taste
4 tablespoons of marshmallow fluff for topping

SERVES 4

BAKED CRANBERRY BEANS
WITH CRANBERRIES

NOTE: The beautiful red and white cranberry beans available in most organic markets inspired Liz's take on this traditional baked bean recipe. Why not combine the beans with dried cranberries for a great cold weather side dish? This makes a perfect "carry-in" dish for a pot luck as well.

(1) Cover the beans with cold water in a cast iron enameled Dutch oven large enough to hold them.

(2) Run your fingers through the beans and discard shriveled beans or pebbles. (Do not salt the water, as this will toughen the beans.)

(3) Bring the water to a boil over medium-high heat; boil for 2 or 3 minutes.

(4) Remove beans from heat and allow to rest for 2-3 hours. Drain beans and discard liquid.

(5) Place the beans back in the Dutch oven and cover with fresh cold water, and once again bring to a boil.

(6) Reduce the heat to medium and simmer until beans are tender to the bite (about 1 hour).

(7) Add the salt to the cooking water once the beans are tender.

Preheat the oven to 350° F.

(8) Drain the beans reserving the cooking liquid.

(9) Place the beans in a 9x12-inch cast iron or glass baking dish. Add the onions, apples, cranberries, and bacon; mix thoroughly.

(10) In a 2-cup glass measuring cup, combine the brown sugar, molasses, cider vinegar, mustard, red pepper, ginger, allspice, and enough of the reserved bean liquid to equal 2 cups. Pour this mixture over the beans and mix again.

(11) Cover the pan with aluminum foil and crimp the edges to seal. Place on the center shelf of the preheated oven and bake undisturbed for 1 hour.

(12) Remove beans from oven and reduce oven temperature to 350° F. Lift the foil from a corner facing away from you as the hot steam will rush out.

(13) Check the level of the liquid, adding more bean cooking liquid if a great deal has evaporated.

(14) Recover the beans with the foil and return to the oven for 1 hour longer.

(15) When the beans have baked for another hour, remove the pan from the oven and remove the foil.

(16) Taste a bean for tenderness and return the pan to the oven for a while longer if necessary.

▨ INGREDIENTS

1 pound of dried cranberry beans
water to cover
2 teaspoons of salt
1 large yellow onion, peeled and diced
1 large firm apple, cored and diced, but not peeled
1 cup of dried cranberries
1/4 pound of diced bacon
1/2 cup of firmly packed dark brown sugar
1/4 cup of dark molasses
1/4 cup of cider vinegar
2 teaspoons of dry mustard
1/2 teaspoon of crushed red pepper
1 teaspoon of ground ginger
1 teaspoon of ground allspice
reserved liquid from cooking beans

SERVES 12

CRANBERRY HAZELNUT BREAD

NOTE: *This loaf makes wonderful toast and the cinnamon, which is "yeast-friendly" aids in the yeast's development, as well as the shelf-life of the bread– if there's any left!*

(1) In the bowl of a heavy duty stand mixer fitted with the dough hook, whisk together the yeast, 1/2 cup warm water, sugar, and cinnamon. Allow to proof for about 10 minutes, or until a grey cap of foam forms on the top of the mixture.

(2) Add the cooled cranberries and their liquid (making sure than they are no more than 115° F.), the remaining 1 cup warm water, and the sea salt. Whisk to combine.

(3) Stir in the whole wheat flour. Place the bowl on the mixer and begin kneading, adding the unbleached flour, 1 cup at a time, until the dough forms a thick mass which begins to stretch from the sides of the bowl. (Note: Do not allow the dough to become so heavy that it completely cleans the sides of the bowl. Keep it wet. With the mixer on low speed, add the cooled hazelnuts. Mix to combine thoroughly.

(4) Place the dough in a large bowl which has been coated with vegetable oil. Cover with a clean linen or cotton dish cloth and set aside to rise until doubled in bulk.

Preheat the oven to 400° F.

(5) Turn dough out onto a floured cloth and cut into 4 equal portions.

(6) Pinch edges together to form a round loaf, deflating the dough as little as possible. Coat the tops with the flour and invert the loaves on parchment-covered pans.

(7) Allow to rise again for about 20

minutes. Slash an "X" in the top of each loaf with a sharp knife.

(8) Place pans in the preheated oven and bake for 15 minutes. Reverse the pans if they are one over the other, and bake for another 15-20 minutes, or until loaves sound hollow when tapped.

(9) Remove to racks to cool.

* *Most of the brown skin can be removed from toasted hazelnuts by rolling them vigorously in a terry cloth towel as soon as they are removed from the oven.*

◈ INGREDIENTS

1 cup of dried cranberries, covered with 1 cup of water, brought to a boil, then removed from heat, reserved

1 cup of shelled hazelnuts *, toasted in a 300° F. oven for 10 minutes, brown skins removed, cooled.

1 tablespoon of granulated yeast

1/2 cup + 1 cup of warm water (not more than 115° F.)

1 teaspoon of ground cinnamon

1 tablespoon of sea salt

2 cups of stone-ground whole wheat flour

5-7 cups of unbleached flour

(vegetable oil for coating bowl)

MAKES 4 LOAVES

ORANGE/CRANBERRY
WHOLE WHEAT LOAVES

NOTE: *Think Thanksgiving! Think autumn squash bisque and these loaves in front of the fire, for Sunday night supper! And think cinnamon toast for breakfast, if there is any left! These traditional fall flavors come together beautifully in these easy-to-make loaves. Organic dried cranberries are a great staple to keep on hand—as good for eating out of hand as for baking into bread.*

(1) In the bowl of a heavy-duty stand mixer fitted with the dough hook, whisk together the yeast, 1/2 cup warm water, and sugar. Allow to proof for about 10 minutes, or until a gray cap of foam forms on the top of the mixture.

(2) Add the cooled cranberries and their liquid (making sure than they are no more than 115° F.), the orange zest, the remaining 1 cup of warm water, and the sea salt. Whisk to combine.

(3) Stir in the whole wheat flour. Place the bowl on the mixer and begin kneading, adding the unbleached flour, 1 cup at a time, until the dough forms a thick mass which begins to stretch from the sides of the bowl. (Do not allow the dough to become so heavy that it completely cleans the sides of the bowl. Keep it wet!)

(4) Place the dough in a large bowl which has been coated with vegetable oil. Cover with a clean linen or cotton dish cloth, and set aside to rise until doubled in bulk.

Preheat the oven to 400° F.

(5) Turn dough out onto a floured cloth and cut into 4 equal portions.

(6) Pinch edges together to form a round loaf, deflating the dough as little as possible. Coat the tops with the flour and invert the loaves on parchment-covered pans.

(7) Allow to rise again for about 20 minutes. Slash an "X" in the top of each loaf with a sharp knife.

(8) Place pans in the preheated oven and bake for 15 minutes. Reverse the pans if they are one over the other, and bake for another 15–20 minutes, or until loaves sound hollow when tapped.

(9) Remove to racks to cool.

▦ INGREDIENTS

1 cup of dried cranberries, covered with 1 cup of water, brought to a boil, then removed from heat, reserved

zest from 2 large oranges, finely minced

1 tablespoon of granulated yeast

1/2 cup + 1 cup of warm water (not more than 115° F.)

1 tablespoon of sea salt

2 cups of stone-ground whole wheat flour

5–7 cups of unbleached flour

(vegetable oil for coating bowl)

MAKES 4 LOAVES

BRAIDED PUMPKIN/CRANBERRY WREATH

NOTE: All of the traditional pumpkin pie spices, plus the addition of dried cranberries, toasted pecans, and small spicy candied ginger, make these loaves irresistible at a festive holiday occasion. (Added bonus—the kitchen smells incredible while they're baking!)

(1) Whisk the yeast with 1/2 cup of warm water. Add the tablespoon of granulated sugar and whisk. Allow to proof for about 15 minutes, or until a foamy cap appears on the surface of the mixture. Whisk in the remaining 2 cups of water, sea salt, and brown sugar. Add all of the spices and mix thoroughly. Add 2 cups of the unbleached flour and the 16 ounces of pumpkin purée.

(2) Allow to sit until bubbles rise to the surface and mixture is foamy.

(3) Place mixture in the bowl of a heavy duty stand mixer, fitted with the dough hook. Add 4 cups of the remaining flour and mix thoroughly. Place the bowl on the mixer and begin kneading with the hook. When flour is completely incorpo-rated, add the cranberries, pecans, and ginger. Continue to knead adding as much flour as necessary until dough is smooth, but still soft. It should just barely clean the sides of the mixer bowl.

(4) Turn the dough out into a large bowl which has been coated with 1 tablespoon of vegetable oil. Cover with a cotton or linen dish towel and put in a warm place to rise. Allow to rise until doubled in bulk (about 1 hour).

(5) Turn the dough out onto a floured surface such as a pastry cloth, and divide with a sharp knife into 6 pieces. Shape the pieces into long ropes of equal length. Braid three of the pieces together, beginning by over-lapping them in the middle and braiding to both ends.

Twist the braid to form a circle and intertwine the ends. Repeat with the remaining three ropes. Place each of the braided wreaths on baking sheets lined with parchment. Allow to rise for about 1/2 hour.

Preheat the oven to 400° F.

(6) Brush the braids with the egg and water mixture. Sprinkle generously with the pärl socker, and bake in the preheated oven, alternating the trays after 15 minutes, until loaves are golden brown and echo when tapped with your knuckle. (About 45 minutes.) Remove to racks and cool.

* *Available from baking supply catalogs such as King Arthur Flour, PO Box 1010, Norwich, Vt. 05055*

▧ INGREDIENTS
1 tablespoon of dry yeast
1/2 cup + 2 cups of warm water (not more than 115° F.)
1 tablespoon of granulated sugar
6 tablespoons of dark brown sugar
1 tablespoon of sea salt
1 tablespoon of ground ginger
1 teaspoon of freshly grated nutmeg
1/2 teaspoon of ground cinnamon cloves
1 teaspoon of ground allspice
1 16-ounce can of pumpkin purée (not pumpkin pie filling)
6-8 cups of unbleached flour (more if needed)
1 cup of dried cranberries
1 cup of pecan pieces (toasted for 10 minutes in a 300° F. oven, then cooled)
1/4 cup of candied ginger, snipped into 1/4-inch pieces

FOR GLAZING
1 egg whisked with 1 tablespoon of water
4 tablespoons of pärl socker (German pearl baking sugar*)

MAKES 2 BRAIDED WREATHS

HONEY AND DRIED CRANBERRY
GINGERBREAD

NOTE: One of the homiest aromas that can emanate from the kitchen is that of a pan of gingerbread baking. The late Laurie Colwin wrote poetically about it in her memorable food essays for Gourmet Magazine. (Thankfully, these columns are now gathered together in two volumes entitled Home Cooking and More Home Cooking.)

NOTE: Liz used honey* in this recipe making for a lighter gingerbread than those made with molasses. Bake a pan-full on a chilly winter day and wax nostalgic with down-home memories.

Preheat the oven to 350° F.

(1) Melt the lard and set aside. Place all of the dry ingredient in a bowl and whisk with a wire whisk to thoroughly combine. (This step will eliminate the necessity for sifting.)

(2) In a glass measuring cup, whisk the eggs and combine with the buttermilk.

(3) With a wooden spoon, mix the buttermilk and egg mixture into the dry ingredients.

(4) Add the lard and honey and stir to combine. Fold in the dried cranberries.

(5) Butter and flour a 9-inch square baking pan. Pour batter into the pan and spread evenly with a spatula.

(6) Place on the center shelf of a preheated oven and bake for 30-35 minutes, or until a tooth-pick inserted in the center comes out clean.

(7) Remove to a rack and cool slightly if you can resist before slicing. Brew a pot of your very best tea and indulge.

While attending the Cranberry Festival and watching the cranberry harvest on Cape Cod in October of 1999, in preparation for this book, Liz met Peter Wilson, a beekeeper who moves his hives from bog to bog during the spring to pollinate the cranberries. The resulting "cranberry honey" can be purchased from him at Cape Cod Cranberry Bog Honey, Peter C. Wilson, 56 Mayflower Ridge Drive, Wareham, Mass. 02571.

▨ INGREDIENTS

1/2 cup of lard, melted and cooled slightly
1 cup of sugar
2 1/2 cups of all-purpose flour
1 teaspoon of salt
1/2 teaspoon each of ground cinnamon, cloves, and mace
1 teaspoon of ground ginger
2 teaspoons of baking soda
2 extra-large eggs, whisked
1/2 cup of buttermilk
1 cup of honey
1/2 cup of dried sweetened cranberries

YIELDS 9-12 SERVINGS

VALENTINE RASPBERRY/DRIED
CRANBERRY SCONES

Preheat the oven to 425° F.

(1) In the bowl of an electric mixer fitted with the paddle attachment combine first five ingredients. Cut in butter until mixture resembles course meal. Add drained cranberries. Whisk together egg and yogurt and add to flour mixture. Mix just until flour is moistened.

(2) Turn dough out on a floured surface and knead lightly until just combined. Divide dough in half. Pat into circles. Place dough circles on a buttered baking sheet and score to create 6 equal wedges.

(3) Whisk together egg and milk. Brush scones with egg wash and sprinkle with sugar.

(4) Place baking sheet on the center shelf of the preheated oven. Bake for 15 minutes or until golden.

(5) Serve with butter, raspberry jam, or sweetened crème fraîche, or whipped cream.

❖ INGREDIENTS

2 1/2 cups of all-purpose flour
1/2 cup of sugar
2 teaspoons of baking powder
1 teaspoon of baking soda
1/2 teaspoon of salt
4 tablespoons of chilled butter cut into small pieces
3 tablespoons of dried cranberries, plumped in simmering water and drained
1 extra-large egg
1 cup of raspberry yogurt

GLAZE

1 extra-large egg
1 tablespoon of milk
2 tablespoons of sugar for sprinkling

MAKES 12 SCONES

MOM'S CRANBERRY SAUCE

NOTE: Once bags of cranberries were in the market, almost no fall or winter meal which Liz's mother cooked ever went without a sauce-boat of this simple, ruby-red sauce to accompany whatever roast, chop or poultry that was served. High in vitamins, potassium and other minerals, cranberries were a very natural, though unconscious, addition to the winter dinner table at the farm. A pot of them seemed to constantly be on the stove, and they perked up the heavy cold-weather meals consisting of large quantities of meats, root vegetables, and baked desserts.

(1) In a heavy-bottomed enameled pot, bring the cranberries and water to a boil over medium-high heat. Reduce heat to a simmer and add sugar. When berries begin to pop and sugar has dissolved, taste for sweetness. The natural pectin in the cranberries, combined with the dissolved sugar will thicken the sauce. When cranberries have mostly burst, remove sauce from heat and cool. Serve in a sauce-boat to accompany roast pork, game or poultry.

▧ INGREDIENTS

1 12-ounce bag of fresh cranberries
water to cover
1 cup, plus or minus, of granulated sugar*

* Note that the amount of sugar will be determined by the sweetness of the berries and your personal taste.

CRANBERRY
BARBECUE SAUCE

NOTE: *This sauce keeps well when covered and refrigerated.*

(1) Put the cider and the tea in a large enameled sauce pan. Bring it to a boil, watching carefully so as not to let it boil over. Reduce heat and simmer until reduced by half.

(2) Add all remaining ingredients. Stir until sugar is completely dissolved and mustard is thoroughly incorporated. Simmer the sauce, stirring from time to time, until the sauce has reduced to about 2 cups. (This might take up to 5 or 6 hours.) It should coat the back of a wooden spoon. Do not be tempted to raise the heat to accelerate the reduction. You do not want to scorch the sauce.

 * *To extract every drop of catsup from the bottle, pour in a little cider and shake well!*

▨ INGREDIENTS

2 cups apple cider
2 cups of strong brewed tea
4 cups of cranberry juice
1/2 cup of balsamic vinegar (ordinary grocery store variety is fine)
1/4 cup of dark soy sauce (May be purchased at an oriental market.)
1/2 cup of dark brown sugar
2 tablespoons of molasses
1 medium yellow onion, chopped
3 tablespoons of minced fresh garlic
4 whole cloves
1 3-inch piece of cinnamon stick
3 bay leaves
1 tablespoon of Worcestershire sauce
2 whole 3-inch long dried chili peppers
2 tablespoons of Dijon mustard
1 cup of commercial BBQ sauce or ketchup*
3 tablespoons of butter

MAKES 2–3 CUPS

GRANDMARNIER
CRANBERRY RELISH

NOTE: Liz purchased her first Cuisinart in 1973 with the check that her mother had given her for her birthday that year. A kitchen revolution was born! One of the chores that was ever-after delegated to her was that of making the cranberry relish for Thanksgiving and Christmas dinners. A snap in the processor! Liz, from the beginning, gussied-up the relish a bit by adding a splash of the orange-flavored Grandmarnier liquor.

(1) Place the cranberries and the oranges, cut into 1-inch pieces, skin included, in the container of a food processor fitted with the steel blade. Process, pulsing on and off, until the fruits are thoroughly chopped, but not mushy Add the sugar and Grandmarnier and pulse to mix. Taste for sugar and add more, if desired. Refrigerate for at least 4 hours to allow flavors to mellow.

NOTE: This jewel colored dish is at its best served in a cut glass bowl which shows off its vibrant color.

◪ INGREDIENTS

1 pound of fresh cranberries
2 large seedless naval oranges
1 cup of granulated sugar (more if desired)
1/2 cup of Grandmarnier liquor

SERVES 8-10

MARMALADE OF
QUINCE WITH CRANBERRIES

NOTE: *Liz first encountered quince in the side yard of her great aunt's house at 417 High Street when she was a child. The bright orange/pink flowers, reminiscent of flowering crab, were a brilliant spring punctuation. In later years she has come across the espaliered trees in gardens in the South of France. Quince is not a fruit that ripens like an apple or a pear. It will remain hard and then rot, but its fragrance is incredible. It also is one of the highest fruits in pectin content, requiring no jelling agent to make a great preserve. Combined with the pectin from cranberries, this is the simplest of natural marmalades. This is a marmalade which is wonderful with toast or brioche, but it works quite well as a fruit compote at breakfast.*

(1) Cover all of the ingredients with cold water in a non-reactive pan such as enamel or cast iron. Bring to a simmer over medium heat. Allow to cook slowly for 30 minutes. Pectin will begin to extract from the quince and cranberries.

(2) Remove the mixture from the heat and measure for volume. Add an equal amount of sugar.

(3) Return to heat and continue to cook for about 30 minutes, or until mixture thickens. DO NOT allow to scorch. Cool.

(4) Place in sterilized jars and refrigerate.

▨ INGREDIENTS

4 quince, peeled, cored and quartered, sliced into 1/2-inch chunks
2 4-inch cinnamon sticks
3 whole cloves
4 slices of fresh ginger the size of a quarter
juice of 1 lime
1/4 teaspoon of lime zest
1/2 cup of dried cranberries
sugar

MAKES ABOUT 6 CUPS

MOM'S BOILED DRESSING

NOTE: This sweet-tart dressing, reminiscent of commercial "Miracle Whip," but made with the readily available eggs and dairy products which Liz's mother had at the farm, was a staple which was always on hand for Waldorf Salads, Cole Slaw, and wedges of head lettuce. Even in later years Margaret would cook up quantities of this dressing to be sold at the annual Graham Hospital Christmas Tea and Bazaar.

(1) Combine all of the dry ingredients and place in the top of a double boiler.

(2) Whisk together the eggs and milk and stir into the dry ingredients. Place over simmering water and whisk constantly. Add the cider vinegar and the butter. Continue to whisk until thickened (about 10 minutes).

(3) Pour into a bowl and cool. Refrigerate covered.

▨ INGREDIENTS

1/2 cup of sugar
3 tablespoons of all-purpose flour
1 teaspoon of salt
1 teaspoon of dry mustard
1/2 teaspoon of ground ginger
1/4 teaspoon of white pepper
1/8 teaspoon of cayenne pepper
2 large eggs
1 cup of milk
1/2 cup of real cider vinegar
1 tablespoon of butter

MAKES ABOUT 1 1/2 CUPS

CRANBERRY
RELISH WITH THYME

NOTE: This savory cranberry relish is the ideal accompaniment to the Salmon with Cranberry Honey (see page 56).

(1) Place the cranberries and the oranges, cut into 1-inch pieces, skin included, in the container of a food processor fitted with the steel blade. Process, pulsing on and off until the fruits are thoroughly chopped, but not mushy.

(2) Add the sugar, thyme, shallot, and Grandmarnier and pulse to mix. Taste for sugar and add more, if desired. Refrigerate for at least 4 hours to allow flavors to mellow.

▨ INGREDIENTS

12 ounces of fresh cranberries
2 large seedless naval oranges
1 cup granulated sugar (more if desired)
2 tablespoons of chopped fresh thyme
1 finely minced shallot
1/2 cup of Grandmarnier liquor

SERVES 8-10

CRANBERRY CHUTNEY

NOTE: *The fragrant combination of cranberries and apples absolutely wafts a potpourri of fall through your house as it simmers. Serve with poultry, pork or game for an autumnal complement to the meat and a radiant burst of color on the plate.*

NOTE: *Find some beautiful hinged French jam jars and make quantities of this to give as holiday gifts. Be sure to keep refrigerated.*

(1) Place all of the ingredients in a medium, heavy-bottomed enameled Dutch oven. (Do not use a metal pan which could react with the acids in the chutney.) Bring to a boil over medium-high heat.

(2) Reduce heat and simmer until cranberries have burst and apple is tender, but not disintegrated. If the liquid evaporates too much, add more water, as needed, in order to keep chutney from sticking. A beautiful deep rose chutney will result.

(3) Cool slightly, and serve over roast quail or other meat. Store the remaining chutney in tightly covered jars in the refrigerator.

▣ INGREDIENTS

1 12 ounce bag of fresh cranberries
1 cup of water
1 cup of unpasteurized apple cider
2/3 cup of brown sugar
1/2 teaspoon each of cumin seed, anise seed, fennel seed, whole yellow mustard seed, crushed red pepper
12 whole cloves
12 whole allspice berries
1 3-inch piece of stick cinnamon
zest and the juice from 2 oranges
zest and juice from 1 lemon
1 large firm apple, cored, but not peeled, cut into 1/4-inch dice
1 teaspoon of Kosher salt
5 cloves of garlic, peeled and slivered
1 medium yellow onion, peeled and diced
2 tablespoons of fresh ginger grated, and juice reserved*
* *A ceramic grater works well for this.*

MAKES 3 CUPS

SPICED CRANBERRY SWIRL

NOTE: Keep this brilliant red syrup in a squeeze bottle in the refrigerator to add a splash of holiday color to everything from a colorful soup to a simple grilled chicken breast.

(1) Place all ingredients in a heavy non-reactive pan such as enameled cast iron. Bring to a boil and reduce heat.

(2) Simmer until cranberries have popped, mixture has reduced to about two cups and is quite thick. (The natural pectin in cranberries allows this to become syrupy.) Cool.

(3) Purée in a blender after removing the cinnamon stick. Push the purée through a sieve to remove any seeds or skins remaining.

(4) Place the cranberry syrup in a plastic squeeze bottle such as a catsup dispenser. Store in the refrigerator.

▨ INGREDIENTS

12 ounce bag of fresh cranberries
water to cover
1 cup of sugar
1 3-inch stick of cinnamon
4 whole cloves

MAKES ABOUT 2 CUPS

QUICK CRANBERRY VINEGAR

NOTE: *Liz normally makes her infused vinegars by the slow process, simply pouring cool vinegar into bottles with the stems of fresh herbs. This hot method will work when you are in a hurry, but do watch the vinegar very carefully when you heat it! You are not out to "stew" your cranberries–simply to extract the flavors!*

(1) Place all ingredients in a heavy enameled sauce pan. Bring vinegar just to the boiling point, over medium heat. Remove pan from heat. Allow vinegar to steep with cranberries and spices until cool, (see note above).*

(2) Divide contents equally between two sterilized decorative bottles. Cork and tie with raffia.

▧ INGREDIENTS

1 cup of fresh cranberries
2 tablespoons of mixed peppercorns (black, white, and allspice)
2 sticks of cinnamon
1 quart of rice wine vinegar (4% acidity)

MAKES 1 1/2 QUARTS

SPICED CRANBERRY COULIS

(1) Place all ingredients in a heavy non-reactive pan such as enameled cast iron. Bring to a boil and reduce heat. Simmer until cranberries have popped, mixture has reduced to about two cups and is quite thick. (The natural pectin in cranberries allows this to become syrupy). Cool.

(2) Purée in a blender after removing the cinnamon stick and the star anise. Push the purée through a sieve to remove any seeds or skin remaining. Add more sugar to taste.

(3) Place the cranberry syrup in a plastic squeeze bottle such as a catsup dispenser. Store in the refrigerator.

▓ INGREDIENTS

12 ounce bag of fresh cranberries
water to cover
1 cup of sugar
1 3-inch stick cinnamon
2 whole cloves
1 teaspoon of dried ginger or 4
   1/4-size pieces of ginger root
1 star anise

NOTE: Like Spiced Cranberry Swirl (see page 82), keep this brilliant red syrup in a squeeze bottle in the refrigerator to add a splash of holiday color to everything from colorful soup to a simple grilled chicken breast.

MAKES ABOUT 2 CUPS

NO-FAIL PUFF PASTRY

(1) Put the flour, salt, and 1 stick of the butter, cut into small pieces, into the bowl of a food processor fitted with the steel blade.

(2) Process until the mixture resembles corn meal.

(3) With the motor running add the cold water through the feed tube until the mixture forms a ball and leaves the sides of the bowl.

(4) Turn the dough out onto a floured pastry cloth and roll out into a rough rectangle about 12x16 inches.

(5) Cut the remaining stick of butter into thirds and refrigerate 2/3 of it.

(6) Cut the first 1/3 into pea-sized pieces and distribute over the surface of the dough. Work quickly to avoid having the warmth of your hands melt the butter.

(7) Use the pastry cloth to help fold the dough like a business letter, 1/3 over 1/3, with the butter enclosed.

(8) Now turn the length of pastry and fold 1/3 over 1/3 to make a compact

▧ INGREDIENTS

2 cups of Wondra Flour
1 teaspoon of salt
2 sticks (1 cup) unsalted, chilled butter
1/2 to 3/4 cup very cold water

package.

(9) Put pastry in a plastic bag and refrigerate for at least 15 minutes. (Do not place in freezer to accelerate chilling.)

(10) Roll at right angles to your rectangle–do not roll diagonally or your butter will not be evenly distributed and you may break through at the corners of the dough.

(11) Repeat from step 6 two more times with the second and third pieces of butter.

(12) At this point the pastry may be used or frozen to reserve for future use.

CRANBERRY COFFEE CAKE

When Liz was a freshman at Simmons College in Boston, she quickly realized that some of the best meals to be had in the dining hall were on Saturday and Sunday mornings! No one got up to go to breakfast on those days! Rashes of bacon, sausage, and freshly baked coffee cakes were all part of the offerings to the meager handful of weekend early-risers. This cranberry coffee cake was really a basic yellow cake with a cinnamon sugar topping, which utilized Massachusetts' most famous agricultural product. Today it still stands out in Liz's mind as one of her favorite food memories at Simmons.

When in Boston during the research for this book, Liz called the college to speak with the current dining hall manager, hoping to trace down the authentic recipe. Sadly, like most colleges today, the dining hall contract had been turned over to a mass-produced food service giant. Though Steve, the food service manager, was more than happy to cooperate, the original recipe for this coffee cake had passed to the "great recipe file in the sky"! This is Liz's recreation of her food memories from the 1960s.

Preheat the oven to 350° F.

(1) Grease a 9x12x2-inch Pyrex baking dish and set aside.

(2) In a large bowl, mix the flour, salt, 1 cup of the sugar, and the melted butter. Add the baking powder, baking soda, egg, and buttermilk. Lightly mix the ingredients. Do not overmix or batter will be tough.

(3) Fold in the cranberries and pour into the prepared dish.

(4) In another bowl, mix the remaining 3/4 cup of sugar and the cinnamon. Sprinkle this mixture over the coffee cake and bake on the center shelf of the preheated oven for about 45 minutes or until just firm and a toothpick inserted in the center of the cake comes out cleanly.

(5) Allow to cool for about 10 minutes, cut into squares and serve.

▨ INGREDIENTS

2 1/4 cups of all-purpose flour
1/2 teaspoon of salt
1 tablespoon of ground cinnamon
1 3/4 cups of granulated sugar
1 1/2 sticks of butter, melted then cooled to room temperature
1 teaspoon of baking powder
1 teaspoon of baking soda
1 egg, lightly beaten
1 cup of buttermilk
1 cup of whole cranberries
1 cup nuts, chopped - optional

SERVES 12

CRANBERRY
CHOCOLATE LAYER CAKE

NOTE: The initial formula for this dense, chocolate layer cake comes from friend Jill Van Cleave, a Chicago restaurant recipe developer and cookbook writer. Liz has varied it to include cranberries for this book.

Preheat the oven to 350° F.

(1) Grease bottom and sides of two 9-inch round cake pans with 1 tablespoon of butter. Add 1 tablespoon of cocoa powder to one cake pan. Tilt and roll the pan to evenly distribute cocoa; shake out excess into the second pan. Repeat to coat bottom and sides of the second pan with cocoa. Shake out any excess. Set pans aside.

(2) Melt 1/2 cup of butter in a glass measuring cup in a microwave oven on high power for 1 minute; or melt over low heat in a small saucepan and set aside.

(3) Sift flour, 1 cup of cocoa, soda, and salt into the bowl of an electric mixer. Add sugar. Turn mixer on to low speed for 30 seconds to combine ingredients.

(4) Increase speed to medium-low. Add buttermilk, coffee, melted butter, eggs, and vanilla. Increase speed to medium and beat about 2 minutes.

Fold in dried cranberries.

(5) Divide batter equally between the two cake pans, filling each about two-thirds full. Bake in middle of the oven until inserted cake tester toothpick comes out clean; and cake is springy when touched, about 35 to 40 minutes.

(6) Set pans on wire racks. When pans have cooled to warm, invert them on cake racks or cardboard rounds. Cool completely before frosting.

Presentation:

(7) Spread a layer of cranberry jelly on one of the cake layers. Top with a layer of Chocolate Butter Cream. Firmly press the second layer on top of the icing. Use a flexible metal spatula to ice the top and sides of the cake. Chill cake to firm icing.

CHOCOLATE BUTTER CREAM

▨ INGREDIENTS

5 ounces of semi-sweet chocolate
1 ounce of unsweetened chocolate
1/3 cup of strong espresso, heated to
  boiling
4 extra-large egg yolks
8 tablespoons of unsalted butter,
  cut into pieces
1 teaspoon of vanilla extract
1 tablespoon of rum

(1) In the container of a food proces-
    sor, fitted with the steel blade,
    process chocolate until fine. (It
    will sound like a machine gun at
    first!) When chocolate is finely
    ground, pour hot coffee through
    the feed tube, with the motor run-
    ning. Add egg yolks, butter, vanil-
    la, and liquor. Process until smooth
    and butter has disappeared.

▨ INGREDIENTS

1 tablespoon of unsalted butter
1 tablespoon of unsweetened cocoa
  powder
1/2 cup (1 stick) of unsalted butter
1 3/4 cups of cake flour
1 cup of unsweetened cocoa powder
2 teaspoons of baking soda
1/2 teaspoon of salt
2 cups of granulated sugar
1 1/2 cups of buttermilk*
1/2 cup of strong coffee
2 large eggs
2 teaspoons of vanilla extract
1/2 cup of dried cranberries
Chocolate Butter Cream
1/2 cup of cranberry jelly for filling

* Buttermilk substitution (for this recipe
    only): Mix 1 cup whole milk with
    1/2 cup sour cream.

SERVES 8 GENEROUSLY

DEEP DISH
PEAR AND CRANBERRY COMPOTE

(1) Place the pear slices and cranberries in a medium enameled Dutch oven and add remaining ingredients. Bring to a boil and reduce heat to simmer.
(2) Cook until pears are tender, but not disintegrated, and liquid has reduced to a syrup. Put mixture in a casserole just large enough to contain it. Cool.

Preheat the oven to 425° F.

(3) Roll out pastry to a thickness of 1/4-inch. With the tip of a sharp knife, trace a lid to fit the top of the casserole. Cut out any desired decorations, such as pears and leaves, from the scraps of pastry.
(4) Place the pastry lid over the cooled pear and cranberry mixture. Brush with the egg glaze.
(5) Position any pastry decorations as desired. Glaze again. Cut slashes in the lid for vents. Bake on center shelf in preheated oven for 35-40 minutes, or until the pastry is golden and puffed, and juices are bubbling.

▨ INGREDIENTS

PASTRY
1/2 recipe of Puff Pastry, reserved (see page 85)

COMPOTE
8 firm Anjou or Bartlett pears, cored, peeled, and cut into lengthwise slices
1 cup of dried cranberries
1 cup of honey
1/2 cup of dark rum
2 tablespoons of ground cinnamon
1 teaspoon of vanilla extract
1 cup of water

GLAZE
1 large egg, whisked with 1 tablespoon of water

SERVES 8

OLD-FASHIONED APPLE/CRANBERRY
CRISP

NOTE: Does anything harken back to the comfort of mother's kitchen like a fruit crisp? Liz remembers these homey winter desserts from the kitchen of the farm 40+ years ago. No boxed mix can ever touch the basic goodness that comes from a dessert like this: seasoned with memories.

(1) Place all ingredients in a large enameled Dutch oven. Bring to a boil over medium-high heat.

(2) Reduce heat and simmer until apples are soft enough to yield when pierced with a skewer, but not so soft that they fall apart. Drain apples and reserve.

Preheat the oven to 350° F.

Topping

(3) Butter a 10x14-inch baking dish. Spread reserved apples and cranberries across the bottom of the dish. Spread the topping evenly over the apples and cranberries.

(4) Bake in the preheated oven for 35-40 minutes, or until topping is browned and bubbling. Remove from oven and serve warm.

NOTE: Accompany with vanilla ice cream or brandy-flavored whipped cream, if desired. Caramel sauce is also wonderful with this.

❖ INGREDIENTS
4 large firm apples, cored and diced
1 12-ounce bag of cranberries
5 whole cloves
2 cinnamon sticks
1 cup of sugar
1 tablespoon of vanilla extract
water to cover

TOPPING

8 tablespoons of butter, cut into 12 pieces
1 cup of dark brown sugar
1/2 cup of oatmeal
1/2 cup of all-purpose flour
1 teaspoon of ground cinnamon
1/2 teaspoon of freshly grated nutmeg

(1) Mix all ingredients together and reserve.

APPLE/WALNUT/CRANBERRY
BREAD PUDDING WITH LEMON SAUCE

(1) Place bread and sugar in a mixing bowl. Pour milk over and mix well. Allow bread to soak up milk for about an hour.

(2) Whisk together eggs, vanilla, rum, and melted butter. Pour over bread cubes.

Preheat the oven to 350° F.

(3) Stir in apples, walnuts, and cranberries, drained of their cooking liquid. Pour entire mixture into a baking dish large enough to hold it. (An enameled cast iron pan with a non-stick finish is ideal.)

(4) Bake in a preheated oven at 350° F. for about 45 minutes, or until puffed and golden. Cool slightly, cut into squares and serve with Lemon Sauce.

▣ INGREDIENTS

4 cups of stale bread, cubed
2 cups of sugar
2 cups of milk
4 eggs
cinnamon and freshly grated nutmeg, to taste
1 tablespoon of vanilla extract
3 tablespoons of rum (Meyers
dark preferred)
3/4 cup of melted butter, cooled
2 Granny Smith apples, chunked
but not peeled
1/2 cup of walnut halves, toasted
1/2 pound of fresh cranberries
cooked for 1/2 hour with 1 cup
of sugar and water to cover,
then cooled.
Lemon Sauce

SERVES 8

LEMON SAUCE

▣ INGREDIENTS
4 tablespoons of unsalted butter
1 cup of sugar
1/2 cup of lemon juice

(1) In a heavy-bottomed sauce
pan, preferably one with a
non-stick coating, melt butter
over medium-high heat.
(2) Add sugar and stir to dissolve.
(3) Allow to caramelize, stirring
constantly.
(4) When sugar is golden brown,
pour in lemon juice.
(5) Mixture will boil furiously and
sugar will seize. Don't be
alarmed.
(6) Continue to stir and sugar will
remelt and sauce will thicken.

MAKES ABOUT 1 CUP

CRANBERRY/BLACKBERRY COBBLER

(1) Use a heavy baking dish, either enameled cast iron or Pyrex. Place berries, apples, sugar, spices, and nuts in dish. Mix thoroughly.

Preheat the oven to 400° F.

(2) Place flour, baking powder, and salt in a bowl. Use a wire whisk to thoroughly mix. With two knives cut butter into mixture until it resembles cornmeal.

(3) Using a fork add egg and milk. Do not over-mix. Just combine ingredients until moistened.

(3) Using 2 teaspoons, drop biscuit mixture evenly over berries.

(4) Place in preheated oven and bake for about 30 minutes, or until biscuit topping is browned and cobbler is bubbling.

▧ INGREDIENTS

1 12-ounce bag of fresh cranberries
4 medium, firm apples, cored but not peeled, diced
1 bag of frozen blackberries
1 1/2 cups of shredded sweetened coconut
1/2 to 1 cup of sugar, depending on sweetness of berries
1 teaspoon of ground cinnamon
good grating of fresh nutmeg
1/2 teaspoon of ground ginger
1/2 cup of toasted almonds or pecans, coarsely chopped

BISCUIT TOPPING

1 cup of flour
1 1/2 teaspoons of baking powder
pinch of salt
1/2 teaspoon of ground cinnamon
4 tablespoons of cold butter
1 extra-large egg
1/3 cup of milk

SERVES 8

PANNA COTTA
WITH CRANBERRY COULIS

(1) In a heavy bottomed sauce pan bring milk and cream to approximately 110° F. Do not allow to boil.
(2) Stir in sugar to dissolve. Add salt and vanilla. Stir in softened gelatin. Gently stir until gelatin has totally incorporated. Remove from heat. Allow to cool until you can place your hand on the bottom of the pan.
(3) Very gently incorporate the sour cream. Pour into one large soufflé dish or eight 1/2-cup soufflé dishes which have been previously rinsed with cold water but not dried.
(4) Refrigerate for at least six hours or preferably overnight.

▦ INGREDIENTS

1 envelope of Knox unflavored gelatin softened in 1/2 cup of cold water (allow to set at least 10 minutes)
2 cups of whole milk
1 cup of heavy whipping cream
1/2 cup of sugar
dash of salt
2 teaspoons of vanilla extract
1 cup of sour cream
Cranberry Coulis for serving (see page 84)

SERVES 8

TO SERVE:

(1) Briefly dip the mold in warm water and loosen Panna Cotta with a flat table knife.
(2) Unmold on serving platter or individual serving dishes.
(3) Surround with Cranberry Coulis.

CRANBERRY CHARLOTTE

NOTE: *This is a winter version of the traditional English summer pudding. It makes a wonderful prepare-ahead dessert for the holidays and may be served accompanied by a custard sauce, whipped cream, or vanilla ice cream.*

(1) Combine cranberries, water, sugar, and spices in a heavy enameled pan large enough to hold them. Bring to a boil, reduce heat and cook until liquid is thick and most of the cranberries have burst. Remove from heat and cool.

(2) Remove cinnamon stick and any other visible spices.

(3) Butter a 2-quart Charlotte mold. Trace the bottom of the mold on one of the slices of bread with a sharp knife.

(4) Butter the round and fit it into the mold.

(5) Remove the crusts from the remaining bread and lightly butter each slice.

(6) Fit the slices upright around the entire mold, overlapping each one as you go. Pour in the cooled cranberry mixture.*

(7) Butter enough of the remaining bread to form a lid for the mold and fit this over the cranberries.

(8) Choose a small plate which will completely cover the mold. Place it on top and weigh it down with something such as a large can of tomatoes.

(9) Place the entire assembly on a large plate with a rim and refrigerate overnight.
(10) When ready to serve, remove weight and plate. Place a serving platter over the mold and invert.

* Any left-over cranberry filling can be refrigerated and used as a sauce.

⊞ INGREDIENTS

2 12-ounce bags of fresh cranberries
2 cups of water
2 cups of sugar
1 3-inch stick cinnamon
3 whole cloves
1 teaspoon of allspice berries
1 teaspoon of dried ginger
1 loaf of Pepperidge Farm thin-sliced bread
1 stick of softened butter (unsalted)

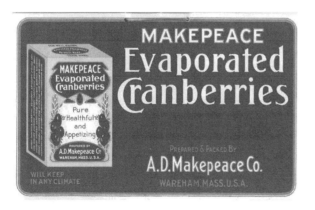

SERVES 10

CRANBERRY/PECAN
CHEESECAKE ICE CREAM

NOTE: *The Inspiration for this "very adult" ice cream came as Liz was developing recipes for this book. Brainstorming for ways to elevate that traditional birthday cake—carrot cake—into something more adult than cream cheese frosting, this cream cheese based ice cream came to be. Long-time cooking class veteran, Joyce Smith, was home from Chicago and came to lunch that day, making her the victim of the official taste test! The results met with her approval, so here is the recipe for you to try! How about à la mode on a still-warm-from-the-oven piece of carrot cake with dried cranberries and pecans? You'll never miss the birthday candles!*

(1) Make a simple syrup by combining the sugar, water, and lemon zest in a heavy enameled sauce pan and bringing them to a boil over medium-high heat. Allow the syrup to simmer for 15 minutes in order to slightly "candy" the lemon zest. Cool.

(2) Plump the dried cranberries in 1/2 cup of the simple syrup. Cool.

(3) In the container of a food processor fitted with the steel blade, process the cream cheese until smooth. Add the simple syrup and process. Scape down the sides and process until smooth.

(4) Add the lemon juice, cranberries, pecans, and rum, if using. Pulse to combine.

(5) Pour into the container of an ice cream maker and freeze according to manufacturer's directions.

⊞ INGREDIENTS

1 cup of sugar

1 1/2 cups of water

zest of 1 lemon (about 2 teaspoons)

1 8-ounce package of cream cheese softened to room temperature

1/2 cup of dried cranberries

juice of 1/2 lemon (small Meyer lemon preferred)

2 teaspoons of vanilla extract

1/2 cup of coarsely chopped pecans, toasted for about 10 minutes in a 300° F. oven, then cooled

2 tablespoons of dark rum (optional)

ice cream maker with necessary ice and salt

MAKES ABOUT 1 QUART

CRANBERRY GRANITA

(1) Combine ingredients. Pour into a cookie sheet. Place in freezer. Freeze until mixture begins to firm. At this stage, scrape surface with a fork every half hour, forming fluffy ice crystals.

⊞ INGREDIENTS

2 cups of Simple Syrup (see below)
2 cups of Cranberry Juice

SIMPLE SYRUP

1 1/2 cups of sugar
2 cups of water

(1) In a saucepan, bring sugar and water to a gentle boil. Reduce heat until bubbles break surface. Simmer 10 minutes.
(2) Remove from heat; cool before using or storing.

LINZER HEARTS

(1) In stand mixer fitted with the paddle attachment, cream butter and sugar.

(2) Add flour and salt and mix well. If dough does not immediately pull together, add cold water, one tablespoon at a time until a ball is formed.

(3) Roll out 1/8-inch thick on a floured cloth.

Preheat the oven to 400° F.

(4) Cut out dough with a 2-inch heart cutter. Place on parchment lined cookie sheets. Cut centers out of half of the cookies with smaller heart cutter.

(5) Bake for about 10 minutes. Cool on racks.

(6) Dust cut-out hearts with powdered sugar.

(7) Spread solid hearts with cranberry jam, and sandwich cut-out hearts on top of them. Serve.

▨ INGREDIENTS

1 cup of softened butter
1/2 cup of sugar
3 cups of flour
1/4 teaspoon of salt
cold water; if necessary
powdered sugar
cranberry jam

MAKES ABOUT 3 DOZEN

COCONUT-CRANBERRY
COOKIES

NOTE: These crisp-chewy cookies prove that dried cranberries are a wonderful foil against the sweetness of coconut. They are a delightful and colorful change from ordinary coconut macaroons. In fact, in the Mother's Day Tea cooking class, Donnalou Cornell pronounced them the "best cookie she had ever eaten"!

(1) In the bowl of a stand mixer fitted with the paddle attachment, cream together the butter and sugar.

(2) Add the egg and vanilla and mix.

(3) Add the flour, coconut, and cranberries and mix on low speed to combine.

Preheat the oven to 400° F.

(4) Line a heavy-bottomed, light colored cookie sheet with the baking parchment. Drop the cookie mixture by heaping spoonful into mounds on the parchment. Leave about 2 inches between cookies.

(5) Bake on the center shelf of the preheated oven for about 10 minutes, or until cookies just begin to brown around the edges. Remove to a rack to cool. Serve.

▨ INGREDIENTS

2/3 cup of butter, softened to room temperature

1 cup of granulated sugar

1 extra-large egg, whisked thoroughly

1 teaspoon of vanilla extract

1 cup of all-purpose flour

1 cup of shredded coconut

1/3 cup of dried cranberries

parchment paper for lining baking sheet

MAKES ABOUT 2 DOZEN

CRANBERRY/WHITE CHOCOLATE FUDGE

NOTE: *A recipe from Sharon Burdick's Pine Hill Bed & Breakfast in Oregon, Illinois. Adapted by Liz Clark.*

(1) Bring the butter, marshmallows, sugar, and evaporated milk to a boil over medium-high heat.

(2) When marshmallows are dissolved, continue to boil, stirring constantly, for exactly 5 minutes.

(3) Stir in chocolate and flavoring and stir constantly until chocolate is dissolved.

(4) Add cranberries and nuts and pour immediately into well oiled molds.*

* *Use decorative gelatin molds for a unique gift presentation.*

▨ INGREDIENTS

8 tablespoons of butter

10 1/2-ounce marshmallows

2 1/4 cups of sugar

1 cup of evaporated milk

4 cups of pure white chocolate (not white coating)

1 tablespoon of vanilla extract or flavoring of your choice*

1 cup of dried cranberries

1/2 cup of any toasted nuts, as desired

* *If you choose to use almonds, you may wish to use almond extract.*

CRANBERRY/CHOCOLATE TRUFFLES

(1) In the top of a double-boiler, over medium heat, melt chocolate. (Do not allow hot water to touch bottom of double-boiler.)

(2) Stir in cream, unsalted butter, liquor, and orange peel. Place chocolate mixture in the refrigerator to chill until firm. (May take up to 2 hours.)

(3) To shape truffles, dip out balls of the chocolate mixture with a baby ice cream scoop. Place a dried cranberry in the center of each ball.

(4) Roll in powdered cocoa to simulate the earth clinging to a real truffle. Chill. Serve. (Will keep, covered, in the refrigerator for up to 2 weeks.)

▣ INGREDIENTS

2 8-ounce packages of semi-sweet chocolate
2 1-ounce squares of bitter chocolate
1 1/2 cups of heavy cream
3 tablespoons of unsalted butter
3 tablespoons of Grandmarnier
1 teaspoon of grated orange peel
36-40 dried cranberries
powdered cocoa for dusting finished truffles

MAKES ABOUT
36 TRUFFLES

INDEX

Traditional Country Life Recipe Books from
BRICK TOWER PRESS

Many thanks for purchasing and reading this book. If you would like to subscribe to our cookery series, please return a post card or letter or email to us and we will send the first book free, followed by the next title each month at 30% off the retail price or just $6.95 a copy with free shipping! Don't forget to include your daytime phone number and payment method.

Other titles in this series:

American Chef's Companion
Chocolate Companion
Fresh Herb Companion
Thanksgiving Cookery
Victorian Christmas Cookery
Apple Companion
Pumpkin Companion
Soups, Stews & Chowders
Fresh Bread Companion
Sandwich Companion
Farmstand-Vegetables

Forthcoming titles:

Zucchini Companion
Pie Companion
Ice Creams
Honey
Corn Companion

MAIL ORDER AND GENERAL INFORMATION
Many of our titles are carried by your local book store or gift and museum shop. If they do not already carry our line please ask them to write us for information.

If you are unable to purchase our titles from your local shop, call or write to us. Our titles are available through mail order. Just send us a check or money order for $9.95 per title with $1.50 postage (shipping is free with 3 or more assorted copies) to the address below or call us Monday through Friday, 9 AM to 5PM, EST. We accept Visa, Mastercard, and American Express cards.

For sales, editorial information, subsidiary rights information or a catalog, please write or phone or e-mail to
Brick Tower Press
1230 Park Avenue
New York, NY 10128, US
Sales: 1-800-68-BRICK
Tel: 212-427-7139 Fax: 212-860-8852
www.BrickTowerPress.com
email: bricktower@aol.com

For sales in the UK and Europe please contact our distributor,
Gazelle
Falcon House, Queens Square
Lancaster, LA1 1RN, UK
Tel: (01524) 68765 Fax: (01524) 63232
email: gazelle4go@aol.com

For Australian and New Zealand sales please contact
INT Press Distribution Pyt. Ltd.
386 Mt. Alexander Road
Ascot Vale, VIC 3032, Australia
Tel: 61-3-9326 2416 Fax: 61-3-9326 2413
email: sales@intpress.com.au